EXPLODING POETRY

EXPLODING POETRY
Baudelaire/Rimbaud

GEORGES POULET

Translated and with an Introduction by

FRANÇOISE MELTZER

THE UNIVERSITY OF CHICAGO PRESS/*Chicago & London*

GEORGES POULET was born in Liège, Belgium, in 1902. He received doctorates in both law and letters at the University of Liège, and has taught at the University of Edinburgh, Johns Hopkins University (where he was chairman of the French Department), and the Universities of Zurich and Nice.

Originally published in Paris as *La Poésie éclatée: Baudelaire / Rimbaud,*
© Presses Universitaires de France, 1980.

THE UNIVERSITY OF CHICAGO PRESS, CHICAGO 60637
THE UNIVERSITY OF CHICAGO PRESS, LTD., LONDON

© 1984 by The University of Chicago
All rights reserved. Published 1984
Printed in the United States of America
91 90 89 88 87 86 85 84   5 4 3 2 1

LIBRARY OF CONGRESS CATALOGING IN PUBLICATION DATA

Poulet, Georges.
  Exploding poetry.

  Translation of: La poésie éclatée.
  1. French poetry—19th century—History and
criticism.   2. Baudelaire, Charles, 1821–1867—Criticism
and interpretation.   3. Rimbaud, Arthur, 1854–1891—
Criticism and interpretation.   I. Title.
PQ431.P6813 1984   841'.8'09   83-18062
ISBN 0-226-67650-1

Contents

Introduction

éclater—to divide; to burst, explode into pieces
éclaté—technical. The graphic representation of a complex object (machine, motor, work of art) which shows its normally invisible parts by the separation of these parts depicted in perspective.

—*Petit Robert*
dictionnaire de la langue française

THE DICTIONARY DEFINITION OF *éclater* gives us not only the full meaning of this book's original title, *La Poésie éclatée*, but the critical ontology of Georges Poulet as well. For it is in this that the greatness of Poulet's writings consists: his ability to take a work of literature and, by separating its parts, to reveal what is normally invisible. Poulet's methodology is in this sense a dissection—the separation of parts for the purpose of close analysis and examination. But, unlike the analogous laboratory undertaking, which generally presupposes a scrutiny of parts for the purpose of understanding the whole, Poulet's dissection first assumes a whole and then tries to situate the parts it comprises. This "whole" is a single consciousness, of which the work of art presents the multifarious moving parts. As Poulet puts it, "All critical method has for its express mission to make me recognize the primacy of subjective consciousness."[1]

The reader of this book on Rimbaud and Baudelaire should not be surprised, then, that Poulet has written on both of these nineteenth-century poets before. Baudelaire's work in particular has prompted a number of essays by Poulet. But if a literary work, in Poulet's view, needs explosion (éclatement) in order to be at least partially grasped, then any essay on a given author is an independent movement toward an intimacy with the consciousness that

1. As cited in Robert R. Magliola, *Phenomenology and Literature: An Introduction* (Lafayette, Ind.: Purdue University Press, 1977), 22.

vii

informs it. And if the act of reading allows for the invasion of another into the mind of the reader, the critic's project can never be a wholly successful one, since any formulation of the movement within another's consciousness is at best an analogue for both that same consciousness and the experience of reading it. Thus criticism for Poulet attempts to be mimetic of the act of reading. Such a mimesis, moreover, is at once liberating and limiting—limiting because the critic can only try, in a kind of recollection in (partial) tranquillity and repetition of the act of reading, to reproduce the invasion of the reader's consciousness by that of the author; liberating because criticism is the elaboration of the very process of this invasion, allowing me as reader to be the subject of thoughts other than my own. Therefore, says Poulet, "The greatest advantage of literature is that I am persuaded by it that I am freed from my usual sense of incompatibility between my consciousness and its objects."[2]

In reading, then, a division takes place ("to divide" being the first meaning of *éclater*); "the 'I' that I pronounce is not myself."[3] In Georges Poulet's writings, the reader comes as close to experiencing the author as subject, rather than as object, as may be possible. But such a persuasion is a paradox, for it is the suspension of the reader's self that allows the consciousness of the other (the author) to live, to be liberated, inside the reader, as subject. "To understand a literary work then, is to let the individual who wrote it reveal himself to us *in* us. It is not the biography which explicates the work but rather the work which sometimes enables us to understand the biography."[4] With Georges Poulet, the split between consciousness and its objects is overcome only by another split within the reader himself.

As the major figure in the so-called "Geneva school," Poulet presents a criticism of consciousness that has engendered attacks as well as praise from nearly every critico-political camp. This should come as no surprise. Many critics sense a confidence, or complacency, in Poulet's work, which they believe results from a deafness on his part to the recent problematization of the literary experience and of the language of literature. Such critics, however, are misreading Poulet—or reading him too literally—for his

2. Georges Poulet, "The Phenomenology of Reading," *New Literary History*, no. 1 (October 1969):55.
3. Ibid., 56.   4. Ibid., 58.

apparent naiveté stems from his insistence upon a consciously deproblematized love of literature. Such a love is not to be taken lightly, even though my formulation of it might be easily dismissed as platitudinous. It is Georges Poulet's great love for literature that makes his writings both thoroughly engrossing and enormously seductive. It is a love which takes great courage, for it makes Poulet vulnerable to a myriad of more "sophisticated" poststructuralist approaches. Indeed, it is ironic that Poulet has been accused more than once of false "impartiality," for his partiality to the text is so great that he has publicly admitted himself to be incapable of going to the theater to see a play; he would much rather read it.

Is Georges Poulet a phenomenologist? Is he a radical idealist? Does he have a substantialist concept of consciousness? These are some of the questions that critics have answered in the affirmative to level attacks against him. Though this is not the place to catalogue all of the "isms" to which critics have tried to make Poulet belong, it is a measure of his stature that his writings have been the source of such controversy and that his critical method consistently elicits the attempt to categorize him. No major text on modern literary theory omits his name; few resist the attempt to assess his contribution to critical thought; even fewer withstand the temptation to pigeonhole him into some category or another.

Given Poulet's views on consciousness, it follows that most of his essays are devoted to a single author, and probe the mind of that author in a manner so compelling and moving that the reader is invaded both by the consciousness of the author Poulet presents and by the critical consciousness of Poulet himself. If Poulet is guilty, as some critics have claimed, of insisting on the *tota simul* as over the content of individual works, his readers nonetheless emerge from a reading of his essays with a new vision of a writer. If his dense, at times highly abstract writing is often repetitious and vague, the patience of Poulet's occasionally beleaguered reader will be more than rewarded by the dazzling insights this critic gives us. I can think of no twentieth-century French critic whose prose is more compelling, more intellectually pleasurable. For Poulet's criticism is in itself literature.

Poulet has also been attacked for remaining chained to the Cartesian *Cogito*: "As soon as something is presented as *thought*," writes Poulet, "there has to be a thinking subject."[5] And yet his essay on Descartes manifests a subtler and more accurate understanding of the *Cogito* than his critics would grant him. Poulet writes of Descartes, "It does not follow that I need be now that which I have been a short time before."[6] It is in this essay that Poulet speaks of the doubling of being inside itself (*dédoublement de l'être*), of the mind which precedes itself in its new thought. Such a doubling is also, as we have seen, applicable to Poulet's concept of reading: doubling both as mimesis (*retracing* the thought of a Baudelaire or a Rimbaud, repeating their gestures), and as a divided consciousness tracing a movement of thought which is at odds with its anterior thought. Hence Poulet's fascination with Descartes's dream: "Nothing insures that one moment continues into another, nothing guarantees us that something can make the bridge between this moment and the one that follows."[7] Hence Poulet's return to Rimbaud's famous remark, "Je EST un autre" (I IS another). Hence Poulet's obsession, in this text as well, with the state of waking—that moment when the mind, precisely, hovers between two modes of being. Hence his scrutiny of the dark staircases in Piranesi's engravings. And hence, finally and among many other things, his return to Baudelaire's identification with strangers: "It appears," writes Poulet in this text, "that for Baudelaire the real way to get out of oneself and to unite with that eternal stranger (which is what the other always is for us), is to merge with him into his story."[8]

It equally appears that, for Poulet, the real way to get out of oneself is to merge with the author into hi(s)story, thus freeing me "from my usual sense of incompatibility between my consciousness and its objects."[9] The result, for both Poulet and his reader, is a momentary fusing with another consciousness. And if this fusing be mere illusion, it does allow a greater comprehension, not only of the division that occurs inside thought through the act of reading, but of consciousness itself, of which reading is the refraction.

The *Encyclopedia of Philosophy* notes that, for Descartes, *cogitatio* does not merely mean thinking but also means "any form of

5. Ibid., 56.
6. "Le Songe de Descartes," *Etudes sur le temps humain* (Paris: Plon, 1949), 1:16.
7. Ibid., 27.   8. See below.   9. "Phenomenology of Reading," 55.

conscious state or process or activity whatsoever." For Descartes, the *Encyclopedia* continues, "such phenomena as willing and having are equally forms . . . of *cogitatio*." It is in this sense that Poulet's adherence to the *Cogito* might best be grasped. For him, the activity of criticism does not merely presuppose a thinking subject, but a will to grasp that consciousness, a having-to-grasp it. For Poulet, a book is an author's means "of saving his identity from death."[10] A book is then the rebirth of any given consciousness, a rebirth which the act of writing, like that of waking, like that of criticism itself, endlessly repeats.

Here, then, is Georges Poulet's reading of Baudelaire and Rimbaud; his "explosion" of their writing. And it is to Georges Poulet that this translation of his own book is gratefully dedicated: *hommage*.

FRANÇOISE MELTZER

10. Ibid., 58.

Note on the Texts

EXCEPT WHERE OTHERWISE INDICATED, page references to Baudelaire are to the Pléiade edition, *Oeuvres* (Paris: Gallimard, 1961). References in parentheses are to English translations gathered from a number of sources in Charles Baudelaire, *The Flowers of Evil*, selected and edited by Marthiel and Jackson Mathews, revised edition (New York: New Directions, 1963; © 1955, 1962 by New Directions); translators' names appear in the notes. Page references to Rimbaud are to *Oeuvres*, edited and annotated by Suzanne Bernard (Paris: Garnier, 1960). References in parentheses are to *Rimbaud: Complete Works, Selected Letters*, translated, with introduction and notes, by Wallace Fowlie (Chicago: University of Chicago Press, 1966; © 1966 by The University of Chicago). Where no parenthetical page references are given, the translations are mine.

FM

Preface

IF I HAVE PUT Baudelaire and Rimbaud one next to the other in the
same book, if I have set them apart from all other poets by placing
them as close together as possible, it has not been for the purpose
of showing how much they resemble each other. Rather, it is
because what must be recognized is that they differ extraordinarily on almost every important point. My goal is not, therefore, to bring them closer together. It is true that a certain
continuity exists in nineteenth- and twentieth-century lyrical poetry, a continuity by which a lineage can be traced from the
romantics to Baudelaire and Rimbaud, and even to Mallarmé and
the surrealists. The multifaceted character of this continuity is
subtly delineated in Marcel Raymond's excellent book *From
Baudelaire to Surrealism.* It makes it possible for us to discern the
persistence with which certain themes were handed down with
increasing intensity in the course of a century and a half of poetry. Thus it is not incorrect to consider the development of poetry,
during the whole of this period, as an uninterrupted phenomenon in which the poets, great as they may have been individually, are almost equally great by virtue of the constancy with
which, one after the other, they have gone back to certain ways of
inventing and practicing poetry. If we consider all the poetry
extending from the time of the French Revolution to the period
between the two world wars, we can perceive an undeniable
similarity between all major poets of the period. This similarity
might well be compared to the resemblance revealed in family
portraits assembled in the same album. Whoever would write the
history of poetry must be attentive to such resemblances and,
better yet, must find a way of pointing out the consistency of
certain traits among them. That history should attempt to identify as clearly as possible the bond uniting the poets of approx-
imately the same period.

Such is not my intention, however. In my view, on the contrary, remarkable writers of any age are but feebly distinguished by what they have in common and, conversely, strongly distinguished by what separates them. Every important period is characterized primarily by the dissimilarity of the talents that compose it. This clearly diminishes the possibility of producing a historical work, since the principal goal of the latter is to focus on the common traits to be found among people of a given period. What seems more genuine to me, however, is to stress the radical individuality of those who constitute an epoch. In other words, as soon as we seek to reveal the originality of persons taken individually, the resemblances disappear (or become of minor importance). What counts then is the qualitative difference by virtue of which no genius may be identified with another, even with another genius of approximate equivalence.

Instead of a unifying comparison of writers of the same period then, a kind of reverse perspective may be taken, aiming to show the differences among those that have been thrown together. Not that the goal of such an attempt at differentiation is to increase the value of one type of approach at the expense of the other. Nothing could be more futile than an attempt to establish, for example, the superiority of Baudelaire over Rimbaud or vice versa. A certain absurdity, or at least a serious violation of the truth, may also be found in studies that make everything depend upon a common ancestry, and thus upon an alleged analogy, between the two poets. No: the only possible way of achieving a fair treatment of both is to allow their differences to emerge—or, more accurately, their independence. If we seek to understand that brand of miracle, or at least that unforeseeable and almost unhoped-for event, that is always created by the advent of a great poet, there can be no other solution but to put oneself squarely inside his individual world, and to present that world for what it is: totally incompatible with any other. Take Baudelaire and Rimbaud, for example. The former feels harshly predetermined by original sin, which threatens to deprive him of all freedom of thought. He is haunted by the past and by remorse; he perceives in himself only endless depths extending to the farthest reaches of his retrospective thought. The latter, on the other hand, keeps awakening to a new existence. He is exempt from all remorse, free to reinvent his world and Self at any given instant, so that this moment immediately acquires an absolute value for him. Between these two worlds, one of determination, the other of liberty and novelty, there is no resemblance. The only similar trait we might establish between Baudelaire and Rimbaud consists in the reciprocal absence of communication between their two worlds. From this we may conclude that between these two large, self-contained countries, with closed borders, there is indeed the means of creating a type of confrontation, but not the slightest reconciliation, except with respect to a few details. Baudelaire and Rimbaud are such powerfully original minds that there is only one possibility for taking in their two universes with the same glance: to apprehend them, so to speak, in their differences.

One reservation: clearly opposed as they are to one another, there is a point at which Baudelaire and Rimbaud, in more than one context, seem to come together. Unrelenting as Baudelaire's initial determinism may be, it is at times interrupted or modified by sudden experiences that are like succor from another place, and which we can call "grace." His determinism may be affected by certain fits of will, or by combinations of a mind straining to accommodate itself to the rigors of its situation. Thus an aspect of freedom is injected into the cycle of determinist causality that governs the Baudelairean world—and perhaps an element of chance as well and, consequently, of hope. Precisely the opposite occurs in the Rimbaldian world. He keeps starting anew from his "awakening," that is, from his Self prepared to reinvent itself from top to bottom at any given moment of his existence; yet Rimbaud quickly begins to feel imprisoned by his own inventions. It is as if Rimbaud, a free man above all or, rather, an adolescent intoxicated by his own freedom, had finally become the captive of an endless circle of thoughts and images that beleaguered him, yet of which he was the sole author.

One last remark. I have tried to show that Baudelaire and Rimbaud represent two opposing tendencies: one seeing the hand of fate everywhere, and the other demonstrating in every act the role of creative freedom. It should be recalled that the same opposition can be found scattered throughout literature. Racine and Corneille, Balzac and Stendhal, the naturalists and the symbolists—all generally represent two alternatives: one consists in imagining the external and internal worlds as ruled by the determining power emanating from a general causality, whatever it might be; the other represents human thought as itself freely creating the situations in which it chooses to find itself. If we pass quickly from one author to another, the mental universe presented by the first crumbles, leaving an entirely different one in its place, irreconcilable with the universe it confronts. It is in this sense that from Baudelaire to Rimbaud there occurs what we may term an explosion of poetry.

Baudelaire

I

WHO AM I—I, Baudelaire? The answer to this question, constantly put forth by the poet, is always instantaneous and the same: I am a man, that is to say, a fallen being, ashamed of existing, doing evil, trampling in mud that is no different from me. Moreover, in my misery as in my baseness I discover that I am a poet. But a poet is no different in kind from other men; he is simply one in whom the repulsive traits common to all men are most clearly in evidence, thus inspiring from first glance a more vivid sense of horror. I, Baudelaire, because I am a poet, am eminently representative of human vileness. My situation is unexceptional, but the consciousness I have of it is in itself exceptional. Not for an instant do I forget the fact that my nature, like that of the entire human species, is one of degradation, and that the mud in which I trample fills a place essentially low and dark—a place into which the whole of creation, by reason of a Fall that occurred at its origin and irrevocably altered its essence, has forever slipped.

Consciousness of self in Baudelaire is of a complex character from the outset. It is the consciousness of a being who experiences in an extraordinary manner within himself a fate shared by all beings; and it is further a consciousness of that fate as the consequence of a change brought about at the very source of life. It is as if, the instant he was created, the first man and all of his descendants with him had undergone an incomprehensible mutation, such that, for the rest of the time allotted them on earth, men are condemned to be pulled in two opposite directions: conscious of being both the heirs of certain riches, possessors of a certain initial nature, yet dispossessed of that nature and dispossessed of that wealth.

At a certain point in his life, Baudelaire will link this dual and contradictory consciousness of self to a religious belief, that of original sin. His religion, as Marcel Ruff has shown, is an aggravated Jansenism. For Baudelaire, as for the disciples of St. Augustine and Jansen, the natural depravity of man is tied to the belief in an original Fall, which engendered the loss of an initial state of happiness and glory. In contrast to the general denial of original sin—a denial which, in Baudelaire's view, serves as a

3

patent example of the blindness of his age—for Baudelaire there is an opposing predication. Yes, original sin exists: its influence alone can explain the duality found in all men as soon as they examine themselves or look deeply within themselves.

This duality implies heights and depths. Theological space is a chasm. The sinner is he who, because of the burden of his culpability, slides toward and finally falls over the precipice. From that moment on, the only essential relation for him is the one established between two points separated perpendicularly. The Baudelairean being, like the Hugo being, is essentially one who lives the experience of the chasm into which he has plunged. For the author of the *Flowers of Evil*, however, this descent into the abyss does not have the same brutality as the Fall of the human (or angelic) being in Hugo. For Hugo, the Fall is both crushing and without bounds. It is the hideous substitution of the void for plenitude, a tragic manner of being lost in the immensity of a cosmos replaced by its opposite, nothingness. Conversely, in Baudelaire, the descent of the damned occurs almost slowly. It is never too rapid to be registered in some fashion from moment to moment and place to place by the one who is subject to it. Thus the poet can measure at a glance "the vertiginous staircase which engulfs his soul," and if the damned descends "endless staircases without railing" in the dark, he follows its spiral step by step:

> Hence, lamentable victims, get you hence!
> Hells yawn beneath, your road is straight and steep.
>
> *Descendez, descendez, lamentables victimes,*
> *Descendez le chemin de l'enfer éternel*[1].

It goes without saying that the space traveled does not have the rigidly perpendicular quality of vertical space. Baudelaire's damned follows a sloping surface that allows us to see him throughout his progression toward the underworld. His movement from high to low and from good to evil is not without transition. He succumbs, on the contrary, to the allurement of a gentle and yet irresistible incline. It is by degrees that he moves along the path of his destiny.

---

1. "Delphine et Hippolyte," 139 (151–55, Aldous Huxley).

The following text is from a poem written by the young Baudelaire:

> There is a deep well, a symbolic Gehenna,
> Where Debauchery, that vile black queen, reigns.
> Within its walls, an endless staircase uncoils:
> The path taken here is never taken twice;
> Love plunges, strangled by the foul air.
> From step to step, down the spiral
> She will tumble, poor degraded soul,
> Down to those obscure depths, upon which no eye has gazed.

> *Il est un puits profond, symbolique Géhenne*
> *Où trône la Débauche, immonde et sombre reine.*
> *Un escalier sans fin tourne dans ses parois:*
> *Le chemin qu'on y fait ne se fait pas deux fois;*
> *L'amour tombe étouffé dans l'air qui s'en exhale.*
> *De degrés en degrés au bas de la spirale*
> *Elle ira descendant, pauvre être dégradé,*
> *Jusqu'au fond ténébreux que nul œil n'a sonde*[2].

Let us postpone examining the significance of these gloomy depths, though that is the most important of Baudelairean sites, and limit ourselves for now to the descending motion that spirals downward, thus leading the one who follows its meanderings from one extremity of existence to another. One is reminded here of the movement followed by the prisoner of Piranesi's "Carceri." The intinerary to which the Baudelairean damned conforms, leading into the dark expanses described by the poet, makes its way through an essentially Piranesian world. Yet Piranesi's name is never encountered in Baudelaire's work. No matter. It is of no great consequence whether or not the poet was directly influenced by the artist. He was certainly indirectly influenced. As was shown several years ago by Luzius Keller, the Piranesian view of the world left its mark on the greater part of French poetry in the nineteenth century. Nodier, Hugo, Nerval, Musset, Gautier—each, after his own fashion, transposed into verse the visions of Piranesian ruins and prisons. There are huge rooms, their visible dimensions further increased by a series of

---

2. *Œuvres de Jeunesse,* 219.

stairways, along which the same figure—the prisoner or the damned—disappears and reappears, following a path from landing to landing that will lead him to perdition. Baudelaire needed only to delve into the works of the previous or contemporary generation of poetry to find this obsessive vision. Moreover, he could not avoid encountering it at the heart of a work he admired almost above all others—a work he wished to translate and write a commentary upon because he sensed such similarities between the world it evoked and his own mental universe. Indeed, Thomas de Quincey's *Confessions of an Opium Eater* is nothing more than a prodigious rhetorical amplification of the theme of man as prisoner—prisoner of a movement ceaselessly repeated by his thoughts; a movement that seems, in this obsession, to follow an endless staircase that can lead him not to salvation but only to a hellish end. Nothing could be more immediately Baudelairean than this portrait of a wretched soul, less the captive of the walls enclosing him than of the steps he takes attempting to avoid his fate while in fact engulfing himself ever more deeply into its consummation. The Piranesian and Baudelairean worlds are similar. They are mutually illuminating, to the point that the latter seems to be the verbal commentary of the former. This world is essentially that of the abyss; not so much a space into which one falls and dies as an intermediate area between the high and the low, between light and absolute darkness, between hope and despair—a halfway point which, far from linking the extremes, marks the impossibility of establishing any connection between them.

A wholly mental space; a space of a vertigo which comes to light between two parts of the mind, to both of which the roads are blocked.

A space that can also appear in the form of an immense ceiling crowning the dark interior edifice and revealing the total absence of communication between the place from which one departed and that to which it leads:

> I seemed every night to descend—not metaphorically, but literally to descend—into chasms and sunless abysses, depths below depths, from which it seemed hopeless that I could ever reäscend.[3]

3. De Quincey, *Confessions of an Opium Eater* (Boston: Ticknor, Reed, and Fields, 1851), 110–11.

It is indeed vain to hope for a climb back up to the daylight, for a screen blocks the light from the self, preventing light from triumphing over dark. "No eye from heaven can penetrate"[4] the place into which the Baudelairean being sinks. An enormous lid extends everywhere above him. At times it appears as a veil, which the mind draws across the ideal place it dreams of, because it can no longer tolerate contemplating that place: "O ends of autumn . . . —my love and gratitude I give you, that have wrapped with mist my heart and brain as with a shroud, and shut them in a tomb of rain."[5] A song of praise that in fact is a statement of despair. Passionately as the Baudelairean persona may at times wish to accept a fate that condemns him never again to climb back to the daylight, that separates him forever from his ideal and his joy—he cannot help seeing himself lying at the bottom of a tomb. The macabre quality of the tomb is not the principal reason for which Baudelaire chooses to remain in it. The burial vault is not solely a place of unfathomable sadness, "into which enters no rosy or gay beam of light";[6] It is even more the place outside of which, beyond reach, everything rosy and gay is to be found. Thus the Baudelairean being's sliding descent into the abyss has the result of creating a transcendence above the abyss. A transcendence whose presence, remote, inaccessible, and utterly foreign to that which it transcends, can conceive of itself only as the confirmation of an essential difference between the transcender and the transcended. Such are the "vanished coconuts of hidden Africa," of which the negress's hagard eye dreams, "behind the thickening granite of the mist."[7] Thus the ceiling, the curtain, the veil, the lid assert themselves as a closure beyond which the happiness lost is to be found. At times the density is such that it creates something like negative depth, a distance at once spatial and temporal, too vast for the mind to hope ever to cross. This distance is the past; not the past lost and dreamed of, in the age before the Fall, but rather the past that has elapsed since the Fall, the evil past. It extends backward like the open country of an existence irrevocably polluted over its entire expanse. Nothing is more rigorously imagined by Baudelaire

4. "L'Irrémédiable," 75 (98, Henry Curwen).
5. "Brumes et pluies," 96 (128, Edna St. Vincent Millay).
6. "Les Ténèbres," 36 (48, Lewis Piaget Shanks).
7. "Le Cygne," 83, (109, Anthony Hecht).

than this system of two pasts—one radiant and paradisiac, followed by another, dark and irreparable.

Baudelaire is the poet of irreparability, that is, of remorse:

> How shall we kill this old, this long Remorse
>   Which writhes continually
> And feeds on us as worms upon a corse?

> *Pouvons-nous étouffer le vieux, le long Remords,*
>   *Qui vit, s'agite et se tortille,*
> *Et se nourrit de nous comme le ver des morts?*[8]

The past to which remorse is connected is not the happy past, the one directly evoked by a nostalgic thought. What is rather remembered here is an indelible series of errors by reason of which, in the span of one lifetime, an individual has completed his downfall and forever parted with his portion of the inheritance. And the mnemonic image which for Baudelaire reigns immutable, at the gates of mental life is one of a decayed beauty, of a soiled happiness; flowers of evil, in the sense that the flower of good and happiness has disguised itself as its opposite. It is a memory of the senses, at times even of the flesh, for what is almost always preserved is an experience inscribed on the body as it is on the soul of whoever has been its subject. In any case, Baudelaire never ceases being haunted by his bad past, that sinister self-portrait which, like a curse or stigma, follows him throughout his life. "I am like a wearied man who looks back and can only see, in the depth of years, disillusionment and bitterness."[9]

These "deep years" are often mentioned by Baudelaire. Depending upon the context, they designate affective worlds, each very different, which embrace extreme sadness as well as extreme joy. But in all of the numerous cases in which the poet measures this oscillation, the result for him is a characteristic dilation of the consciousness of self. For Baudelaire, existence manifests itself in the guise of an immense continuity, seen from a receding perspective in which an individual recognizes himself all the way along. I, Baudelaire, am not simply the moment I am presently living. I am a line that projects itself and, in so doing, is not obliterated along the path already traveled. Surely this is why

---

8. "L'Irréparable," 52 (69, Sir John Squire).   9. "Fusées," 1264.

Baudelaire attempts simultaneously to recall and to flee his past. On the one hand, he has no choice but to recall it, since to live is to become endlessly, retrospectively conscious of the transformation of the present into elapsed time. On the other hand, how horrible it is to discover that one cannot modify even the most insignificant of past events. More than anyone else, Baudelaire has a vivid sense of the process of immortalization by which all that slips into the past is paralyzed in it forever. The poet of remorse is then also the poet of irremediable time, time lacking in all freedom of being. It is a time that fossilizes as it passes from the present into the category of time elapsed. Consequently, in one form or another, whether as the damned descending the stairs without a bannister, whether as a ship trapped in polar icebergs, but always a slave to fate—Baudelaire offers himself as the victim of some diabolical Destiny, which, having assigned him an irrevocable lot, never tires of watching over him to ascertain that it is executed in all of its severity, with neither abatement nor mitigation.

Henceforth Baudelairean time will most often manifest itself in the form of a time fixed in advance and entirely contained in its previous segment. Neither the present nor the future can ever prevent the *stoppage* of time. Time is no longer a becoming; it is a continuing state. "There are eternal situations," says Baudelaire," and everything having to do with the irremediable falls into that category."[10] Eternal situations are those in which the future and present cannot be distinguished from the past that determines them. Consequently there is in Baudelaire a perspective by which the depth of existence is merely the unfolding of an identical human landscape as far as the eye can see. One is reminded here of Mallarmé's swan, frozen forever in the same position, for the landscape reflects the same undefined, monotonous quality; it is a time trap from which all desire for escape is futile. It is no doubt to this particular type of lived time that Baudelaire alludes when, in a letter written to his mother in 1876, he tells her of the "continuity of horror" he glimpses before him.[11] And it is assuredly with the same outlook in mind that

10. "Les Paradis artificiels," 436.
11. "A sa mère," 6 May 1861. Letters to Baudelaire's mother are collected in *Lettres à sa mère* (Paris: Calmann-Lévy, 1932). The general correspondence is in the Pléiade edition, *Correspondance*, 2 vols. (Paris: Gallimard, 1973).

Baudelaire—confronted several years earlier by the guardian who imposes upon him indefinitely the same restrictions and obligations—feels himself overcome by a nameless rage, complete with vomiting and vertigo. He writes: "I saw before me an endless series of years without family, without friends, without the friendship of a woman . . ."[12]

The irreparable is thus the interminable. It is the transformation of time into a sinister eternity, similar to the privative time span, frozen within itself, which is the punishment reserved for the damned. In the general universe of their existence, the damned have a single preoccupation: remembering their unalterable past. Such is remorse. It becomes the single element of thought, the exclusive object of the mind's activity.

Baudelairean time may also be viewed as a perpetuity, but of a special and particularly malevolent type; a destructive perpetuity. "My soul is prey to the Irreparable/It gnaws with tooth accurst."[13] In one sense, time appears to be immobile, since it cannot be altered. In another sense, it reveals itself to be the incessant annihilator of everything it contains. The essential process suggested by the act of gnawing is one of an imperceptible but tireless destruction of being. Somewhere, Baudelaire writes: "Time eats life," and then adds immediately that this dark enemy "preys upon the heart."[14] Elsewhere he says that man is "blind, and deaf, and like a wall unsteady/Where termites mine the plaster."[15] Or, once again: "As the immense snows a stiffened body hide/So Time devours me momentarily."[16]

Thus time is at once frail as an insect and vast as space. On the one hand it is reduced to the corrosive activity of a minute creature. On the other, it is magnified to the proportions of total space, where there is no longer time because there is no longer movement. This ultimate disappearance of time merging into the uniformity of space fires Baudelaire's imagination. He describes this moment as a gradual slowing down of things:

> I envy the least animals that run,
> Which can find respite in brute slumber drowned,
> So slowly is the skein of time unwound.

12. "A sa mère," 11 September 1856.
13. "L'Irréparable," 53 (70, Sir John Squire).   14. "L'Ennemi," 16.
15. "L'Imprévu," 154 (199, Roy Campbell).
16. "Le Goût du néant," 72 (95, Barbara Gibbs).

Je jalouse le sort des plus vils animaux
Qui peuvent se plonger dans un sommeil stupide,
Tant l'écheveau du temps lentement se dévide![17]

The immobilization of time thus produces the same effect as the unification of space. The consequence of both is an intense feeling of ennui. Baudelaire's ennui ressembles the tormenting deprivation of the individual, which is Pascal's ennui. It is not unlike the inertia or lethargy which lies in wait for the *homme sensible* of the eighteenth century. But it is also a very tangible notion: the persistence of a state rendered insufferable by dint of its invariability. Even more, it is the consciousness of this invariability, that is, of the irrevocable quality of fate. The result is that, on the one hand, the Baudelairean being recognizes the immutability of his lot with increasing intensity; on the other hand, he strains to repress his awareness of that lot—hence his desire to find refuge in a dreamless sleep. The ennui described by Baudelaire is thus a complex form of experience. It is a maximum of consciousness in a minimum of action; or, more precisely, it is a maximum of consciousness which has as both its cause and its effect a minimum of action. Seen from the perspective of this intensification of consciousness, and in the absence of all other activity, time becomes intolerably long:

Nothing can equal those days for endlessness
When in the winter's blizzardy caress
Indifference expanding to Ennui
Takes on the feel of Immortality.

Rien n'égale en longueur les boiteuses journées,
Quand sous les lourds flocons des neigeuses années
L'ennui, fruit de la morne incuriosité,
Prend les proportions de l'immortalité.[18]

A feeling of heaviness is connected to time's length. The poet wants to find some occupation which will take "Time from his slothfulness, the world from spleen" ("et les instants moins lourds").[19]

But all in vain! "Each moment, we are crushed by the thought and feeling of time."[20] The result of a consciousness greatly

17. "De profundis clamavi," 31 (40, Desmond Harmsworth).
18. "Spleen," 69 (91, Anthony Hecht).
19. "Hymne à la beauté," 24 (31, Dorothy Martin).
20. "Mon Coeur mis à nu," 1266.

heightened by time is not only further elongation, but greater heaviness as well. Time is essentially heavy. It makes itself felt through a paralyzing pressure; and if it is true that it activates the powers of the mind, it also concomitantly atrophies any creative power. After Vigny, Lamartine, and Nerval, before Mallarmé, Baudelaire is one of the French poets who has suffered the most from sterility: "I felt myself beset," he writes, "with a type of Gérard-like [Gérard de Nerval] illness, to know the fear of no longer being able to think or write a single line"[21]—"the fear," he continues, "of seeing the admirable poetic faculty, the distinctness of ideas, and the power of hope which in truth make up my capital—of seeing them used up and endangered, and seeing them disappear in this hideous existence rife with shocks and jolts."[22]

In short, impotence arises very early on in Baudelaire's life, "terrible, impassable, like the polar glaciers."[23] This wholly negative feeling never leaves him, and always will tend to increase its sterilizing power. Thus monstrously, the dualism of the poet's spiritual life is furthered: he is simultaneously conscious of himself and conscious that this self of his does nothing, is nothing, and can only be an absence of being.

Hence the need in Baudelaire to restore a type of unity for himself by annihilating one of the opposing tendencies within him.

The desire to sleep forever is for him "a vile and disgusting wish, but a sincere one."[24] "There are times when I suddenly want to sleep eternally."[25] "I want to sleep! To sleep rather than live!"[26] "Resign yourself my heart, poor beast, sleep sound."[27]

This resignation, which is a renunciation, pushes him as far as to dream of suicide. One day when he is contemplating killing himself, he writes a very beautiful and very lengthy letter, the essence of which is that he is ending his life because he can no longer endure living, because "the fatigue of falling asleep and the fatigue of waking up are too much for him to bear."[28]

21. "A Poulet-Malassis," March 1861.   22. "A sa mère," 1 April 1861.
23. "Les Paradis artificiels," 425.   24. "Projects de préface," 189.
25. "A sa mère," 26 March, 1853.   26. "Le Léthé," 140 (42, Doreen Bell).
27. "Le Goût du néant," 72 (94, Barbara Gibbs).
28. "A Ancelle," 30 June 1845.

Only an uninterrupted sleep would seem tolerable to him. But sleep is never entirely uninterrupted. Dreams emerge, giving away secret yearnings. And after dreams in sleep there are also daydreams. As Sartre has pointed out, Baudelaire always wants to be elsewhere; elsewhere than in his inertia, elsewhere than in his remorse, elsewhere than in the awareness of his degradation. To dream of being elsewhere is thus at the same time to dream of being other, to dream of having another self, another temperament, in a different place. Baudelaire's obsession with traveling is more than geographic in nature. His most fundamental desire is to achieve an eschatological displacement. We shall see this more clearly below, when we examine the means by which Baudelaire attempts to flee his essential condition—the state of being of a fallen nature. The dream of happiness which transports him to an imaginary India or Holland ideally transfers him to a place where it seems to him permissible to rediscover himself such as he was or was to have been before the Fall, in the state that theologians call "pure nature." Without for the moment pausing to examine these voyages whose destination is an allegorical country, let us nonetheless note that the Baudelairean voyage, including the mental one, lacks a destination as well as a time span; for "the true voyagers are those who move/simply to move."[29] They go they know not where. And if, in the end, they choose death as their final destination, it is because it is not a concrete destination. It is not a determined or determinable *place*. It is simply an *over there*, as different as possible from the loathed *here*: "The first inn encountered"[30]—"the place from which you will be absent."[31]

In short, the essentially wandering character of Baudelairean thought is lacking in all finality, that is, in all well-defined ideality. This brand of thought attempts in no way to conform—as does Lamartine's, for example—to a preexisting model of an eternal idea, which anticipates the thought as a goal to be reached. Nothing could be less Platonic than Baudelairean thought. It does not project into the future a predetermined paradigm of beauty and happiness, which it then attempts to catch up with in order to conform to it. In fact, the more serious problem is that

29. "Le Voyage," 122 (179, Robert Lowell).   30. "Les Projects," 266.
31. "Les Bienfaits de la lune," 290.

Baudelaire has the greatest difficulty in giving this future any positive aspect. If we exclude a few recurrent dreams, of which we will speak in the second part of this essay, we must conclude that Baudelaire proves himself incapable of a clear conceptualization of any future whatever. For him, the future is simply the possibility of extracting himself from the crushing burden of the present, and to clear at one bound the temporal conditions of existence. Thus the elsewhere and the future are above all centrifugal in function; a pure *beyond (au-delà)*, characterized by the total absence of characteristics:

> Above the valleys and the lakes: beyond
> The woods, seas, clouds, and mountain-ranges: far
> Above the sun, the aethers silver-swanned
> With nebulae, and the remotest star,
> My spirit! with agility you move . . .
>
> Come, travel with me in dreams,
> Far, far beyond the range of the possible and the known!

> *Au-dessus des étangs, au-dessus des vallées,*
> *Des montagnes, des bois, des nuages, des mers,*
> *Par-delà le soleil, par-delà les éthers,*
> *Par-delà les confins des sphères étoilées,*
> *Mon esprit, tu te meus avec agilité . . .* ,[32]

> *Viens! oh! viens voyager dans les rêves,*
> *Au-delà du possible, au-delà du connu!*[33]

It is clear that in these two examples (to which one could easily add many others), the mind's motion has as its function neither a participation in cosmic movement nor a self-elevation which might permit it better to embrace the latter. Baudelaire is in no way a poet of the cosmos. He is neither a Dante nor a Milton. He is even less a Lamartine, in whose works poetic movement tends to accompany things in their ascension and flight. In Baudelaire, movement is the mind's flight *far away* from things and simultaneously away from the place where, in the midst of things, the mind risks finding itself forever trapped. In a word, by virtue of his very movement—which is a movement of horror in the face of

32. "Elévation," 10 (11, Roy Campbell).
33. "La Voix," 153 (190, George Dillon).

14

his present existence—Baudelaire hastens to put as much space as he can between himself and himself. Only through estrangement can he succeed in tolerating himself.

One of Baudelaire's great themes is looking at an object from the greatest possible distance; that is, in spatial or temporal depth, at the edge of the horizon. Speaking of Poe's poems or short stories, Baudelaire notes, "*At the limits of their horizon*, oriental towns and edifices appear, vaporized by the distance, showered by the sun with rains of gold."[34] In an example such as this, the idealization of the landscape depends concomitantly upon a distancing, which makes objects more vaporous, and upon a solar action of disintegration which, drenching the whole of everything in a golden rain, transforms this whole into a multitude of glittering flakes. The sun-star and pure distance collaborate to make objects lose their quality of distinctiveness and to force them into a common background in which they are blurred.

Perhaps the same is true for Baudelairean sunsets as well. Their function is to use distance to engulf not only the light of day but, with it, everything it illuminates: first external objects, and then the mental objects that haunt thought. Thus the sunset is also the setting of human consciousness, its entry into a region of drowsy revery where thought seems gradually to be emptied of its contents:

> Look, the dead years dressed
> in old clothes crowd the balconies of the sky.
> Regret emerges smiling from the sea,
> the sick sun slumbers underneath an arch,
> and like a shroud strung out from east to west,
> listen, my Dearest, hear the sweet night march!

> *Vois se pencher les défuntes Années,*
> *Sur les balcons du ciel, en robes surannées;*
> *Surgir du fond des eaux le Regret souriant;*
> *Le Soleil moribond s'endormir sous une arche,*
> *Et, comme un long linceul traînant à l'Orient,*
> *Entends, ma chère, entends la douce Nuit qui marche.*[35]

---

34. "Edgar Poe," *Oeuvres complètes de Charles Baudelaire* (Paris: NRF, 1928), 9:15–45.
35. "Recueillement," 174 (201, Robert Lowell).

We seem here to be participating in the very creation of distance, or, what amounts to the same thing, the past. For the most part, the Baudelairean past inhabits the mind in the form of a present past, an eternally living past, which persists in weighing down the mind conscious of it. This present past maintains by its very presence a terrifyingly vivid quality. As we have seen, it is indelible. Such is remorse—intolerable because it preserves in the mind an image that remains all too close and, consequently, a burning presence. And yet, Baudelaire wonders, is it not possible to make this past recede into the background of one's perspective? Then its bitterness will be softened, its cruelty rendered less harsh. In the Baudelairean phenomenon of the sunset we witness this kind of *mise au lointain,* a distancing of things. The past, and with it the long procession of memories that normally accompany it, solemnly withdraw with the sun, so that the sunset, as Baudelaire writes elsewhere, becomes "the marvelous allegory of a soul, laden with life, which sinks behind the horizon with a magnificent stock of thoughts and dreams."[36]

The beauty of the image suggested here lies in the fact that what seems to sink behind the horizon is not only a fragment of life but the totality of an existence. The depth of the perspective is reflected in the length of the procession moving along it. But that is not all. This spiritual plenitude, this totality of being, is, in one sense, a voyage. Like a ship filled with passengers, it trims its sails for a destination so distant that it will soon be impossible to keep it in view. The dominating impression, then, is no longer that of a present past, continuing to make its heaviness and bitterness felt. On the contrary, the past evoked here is anguishing only because it is receding. The Baudelairean memory can then be painful in two ways: at times because it persists in remaining cruelly present; at times, conversely, because it is perceived as being gloomily engulfed by the nonpresent.

Hence the typically plaintive quality of this second experience. Whereas remorse in Baudelaire is always accompanied by bitterness ("the bitter-flowing bile of my ancient grief"),[37] the contemplation of the past from a growing distance inspires a more

36. "Notes nouvelles sur Edgar Poe," *Oeuvres complètes,* 10:11–35.
37. "Un voyage à Cythère," 112 (163, Frederick Morgan).

tranquil sadness, with softer accents. Nevertheless, the sight of "a far world, defunct almost, absent,"[38] offers the spectator an image of himself that is profoundly painful since the movement slowly lowering him into death is the image of his own life. And in this contemplation of the self from a distance, across the layers of years, there is for Baudelaire something analogous to a farewell addressed to someone never to be seen again. This is the tone that can be detected in the famous lines:

> How far you are O heaven of delicate scent . . .
> The simple heaven full of stolen joys,
> Is it so farther than the China seas?

> *Comme vous êtes loin, paradis parfumé!* . . .
> *L'innocent paradis, plein de plaisirs furtifs,*
> *Est-il déjà plus loin que l'Inde et que la Chine?*[39]

It is indeed with plaintive cries, with a type of modulated sob, that the poet attempts to call back a distant paradise and to animate it with a voice still silver-toned. Nevertheless, the paradise evoked is even farther away than the most distant lands of the Orient. The poet measures the distance separating him from himself, which tends in his eyes to become an absolute distance. Baudelaire is accustomed to those long glances cast over the shoulder. He is the traveler who stops for the night and makes use of the situation to calculate not so much the progress he has made as the span of life already traversed and thus nearly out of reach.

In the poem of the "femmes damnées," Hippolyte's situation is the same:

> With tempest-troubled eyes she sought the blue
> Heaven of her innocence, how far away!
> Like some sad traveller, who turns to view
> The dim horizons passed at dawn of day.

> *Elle cherchait, d'un œil troublé par la tempête,*
> *De sa naïveté le ciel déjà lointain,*

---

38. "La Chevelure," 25 (32, Doreen Bell).
39. "Moesta et errabunda," 61 (80, 81, Hilary Corke).

Ainsi qu'un voyageur qui détourne la tête
Vers les horizons bleus dépassés le matin.[40]

The traveler looking back can be found in numerous passages in Baudelaire's works. In one of the author's earliest poems (probably dated 1840),[41] he speaks of the sweetness of scanning the east for the scarlet hues of a morning long since vanished. Next comes the comment that it is also sweet to "listen to the echoes which sing from behind," that first sonorous image of reverberation which for Baudelaire allow the songs and cries of the past to be heard from afar in the present moment.

There are many more examples. In "Fanfarlo," another early work, the hero Samuel Cramer describes the disillusionment that separates him from past days: "We are all rather like a traveler who has crossed a very large country and every night looks at the sun, which earlier bathed the charms of the road in gold, setting into a flat horizon."[42] Contemplating the past results in a perception of the platitudinous character of one's present existence, as well as the inaccessibility of one's past. Moreover, every immediate experience, by virtue of its intensity, tends to hollow out an abyss between the present and past. This is the case with Hippolyta, overwhelmed by the shock of the Sapphic experience and unable to perceive of her lost naiveté as anything other than the endlessly withdrawing phantom of a being it no longer is. Such is also the situation of the opium eater, his memory both exalted and vaporized by the stimulant to which he has surrendered his mind: "He is the traveler who turns back, in the evening, toward the land traveled that morning, and who remembers with emotion and sadness the multitude of thoughts that filled his mind while he was crossing those regions now evaporated into horizons."[43]

Thus in Baudelaire the experience of depth can be confused with that of the abyss. Evocation is transformed into evaporation. And, far from offering itself, with each occurrence, as a salvation from anguish and sadness, depth in Baudelaire—and mnemonic depth in particular—frequently reveals itself to be the powerful

40. "Delphine et Hippolyte," 136 (151, Aldous Huxley).   41. 193.
42. "La Fanfarlo," 493.   43. "Les Paradis artificiels," 442.

catalyst of despair. In a quatrain from "Balcon," depth appears as an interior void:

> Can vows and perfume, kisses infinite,
> Be reborn from the gulf we cannot sound;
> As rise to heaven suns once again made bright
> After being plunged in deep seas and profound?

> *Ces serments, ces parfums, ces baisers infinis*
> *Renaîtront-ils d'un gouffre interdit à nos sondes,*
> *Comme montent au ciel les soleils rajeunis*
> *Après s'être lavés au fond des mers profondes?*[44]

The answer to this question is sadly negative. In contrast to cosmic phenomena with their inexhaustible power of renewal, psychic phenomena plunge into a chasm in which they cannot find the resources necessary to return full of the vigor they had once possessed. The most important of all experiences in Baudelaire, that of depth, is one not of restoration but of disintegration. It is the disappearance of an existence in that vast, dark region into which all forms of life, thought, emotion, memory, and feeling are soon to sink.

Thus nothing haunts Baudelaire's thoughts more than this immense, eternally gaping interior region. He gives it a name which he even considered giving to his great collection of poetry: "Limbo." Delacroix's painting *Women of Algiers* impressed Baudelaire above all others because he sensed in it affinities with his own mental state. In the painting, he says, he feels "the strong scent of a place of iniquity, which soon guides our thoughts toward the fathomless limbo of sadness."[45] Moreover, the Delacroix painting probably inspired "Hippolyte et Delphine," a poem that presents Sapphic love as the opportunity for its practitioner to discover the abyss of her own thought:

> I feel my inmost being rent, as though
> A gulf had yawned—the gulf that is my heart . . .
> As fire 'tis hot, as space itself profound—

---

44. "Le Balcon," 35 (47, F. P. Sturm).   45. "Salon de 1846," 898.

> *. . . Je sens s'élargir dans mon être*
> *Un abîme béant; cet abîme est mon cœur! . . .*
> *Brûlant comme un volcan, profond comme le vide!*[46]

Aided by Delacroix, who opens "immense vistas to the most adventurous imaginations,"[47] Baudelaire thus discovers (perhaps not exactly, as Sartre would have it), the nothingness to which all consciousness is brought and more precisely, the "depth of perspective"[48] that is revealed each time consciousness sees aspects of spiritual life—which had at first enriched and animated the same consciousness—disappear into that depth. Depth is not pure vacuity; it is rather an interior spaciosity, the place of all mental activity. This spaciosity is most often revealed in the objects thought chooses to contemplate; but at times it may be within thought itself, in the absence of all objects—like the host who, having given a banquet for numerous guests, finds himself alone in the room they have just vacated. The theme of interior depth then, is linked to that of the survival of the mind after the shapes that had temporarily occupied it. This theme in Baudelaire may have come from the works of Poe, in which it abounds and in which one encounters in every utterance the description of a thought solitarily persisting in the tomb. It is the theme of the living dead, a frequent one in Baudelaire as well:

> But tell me if any torture is left to dread
> For this old soulless body, dead as the dead?
>
> *Et dites-moi s'il est encor quelque torture*
> *Pour ce vieux corps sans âme et mort parmi les morts?*[49]

The anguish described here does not come from the fact that, after death, the body of the deceased may be destined to endure new tortures. What is frightening is, rather, that this posthumous torture may include consciousness. Similarly, in calling to mind a figurine by Eugene Christophe, representing a woman hiding her tears behind a mask, Baudelaire asks himself, "But why is she weeping?" He offers himself the following answer:

> She weeps, mad girl, because her life began;
> Because she lives. One thing she does deplore

---

46. "Delphine et Hippolyte," 138 (154, Aldous Huxley).
47. "Salon de 1846," 889.   48. "Salon de 1859, 1083.
49. "Le Mort joyeux," 67 (88, Jackson Mathews).

So much that she kneels trembling in the dust—
That she must live tomorrow, evermore,
Tomorrow and tomorrow—as we must!

—*Elle pleure, insensé, parce qu'elle a vécu!*
Et parce qu'elle vit! Mais ce qu'elle déplore
Surtout, ce qui la fait frémir jusqu'aux genoux,
C'est que demain, hélas! il faudra vivre encore!
Demain, après-demain et toujours!—comme nous![50]

The cause for the sadness expressed here has nothing to do with the objective quality of existence itself. The masked woman is not weeping because of the particular grievances which overwhelm her. She is weeping because the most unbearable of all situations is the one in which life continues indefinitely without in some way being distracted from itself by the events, whatever their nature, that occupy the mind.

In short, at the end of its itinerary, after the series of experiences which it has provided for itself, Baudelaire's thought defines itself in two ways, both similar and opposed: either as pure depth without objects, or as pure activity of mind without reason or end. Who am I, Baudelaire asks. Am I the void I see growing inside me, or am I the movement passing through that void, filling it? Am I to recognize myself in the tragic absence of existence I am leaning over, or in the act by which I conceal this absence from myself?

This is assuredly the furthermost point of thought's movement closing in on itself. Alternatively discovering and fleeing objects, the Baudelairean intellect ultimately finds itself in the presence of a depth that nothing can animate any longer except thought itself: a type of perpetual motion machine running on empty. In this way, to an extent, Baudelairean thought tends to merge with this bare cavity; on the other hand, however, it is capable of seeing itself, vertiginously and in its own mirror, only as a thought which thinks itself, which eternally thinks itself:

The dialogue is dark and clear
When a heart becomes its mirror!

Tête-à-tête sombre et limpide
Qu'un cœur devenu son miroir![51]

---

50. "Le Masque," 23 (29, Graham Reynolds).
51. "L'Irrémédiable," 76 (99, Henry Curwen).

21

2

WHO AM I, Baudelaire wonders. Or, rather: who am I no longer? Consciousness of self is here less a consciousness of who one is than of who one is no longer, from whom one has begun infinitely to differ through the effects of downfall and debauchery. Baudelaire looks at himself in the mirror. Whom does he see in it, if he can still see anything there? A Narcissus never less disposed to forgive his reflection its inferiority, its lack of similarity. The act of consciousness becomes an activity of hatred and, worse still, of ironic disdain:

> I am the ulcer and the lance;
> I am the bruise; I am the blow;
> I am the rack, the limbs also,
> Hangman and hanged at once.

> *Je suis la plaie et le couteau,*
> *Je suis le soufflet et la joue!*
> *Je suis les membres et la roue,*
> *Et la victime et le bourreau!*[52]

Everything leads to the splitting of an existence that contains both the torturer and the tortured; an existence in which thought wreaks vengeance upon itself, out of the shame it feels for being what it has become. But another stance is possible. It consists, not in rejecting one's shame, nor in hurling it with rage in the face of the figure one no longer wishes to be, but, conversely, in accepting shame as the common lot of all those who suffer. Because he knows himself to be fallen, Baudelaire often thinks only of jeering at himself, of self-disavowal. But at other times, precisely because he knows himself to be fallen, he considers himself the representative of a humanity which is itself fallen—that is, deprived of the joy and dignity it might have possessed. To see oneself in this light is, once again, to see oneself doubled. It is simultaneously to see oneself for what one is and to dream oneself into what one might have been. At times such as those, it is no longer self-hatred that reigns, but melancholy. Baudelaire

---

52. "L'Héautontimorouménos," 74 (97–98, Naomi Lewis).

describes melancholy in these terms: "an ardor, a will to live, coupled with a surge of bitterness, as if from deprivation and despair."[53] "When an exquisite poem brings tears to the eyes," he writes further, "these tears are not evidence of an excess of joy; they bear witness, rather, to an aggravated melancholy, a postulation of nerves, a nature exiled in the imperfect that desires to take immediate possession, on this very earth, of a paradise to come."[54]

Melancholy, then, is a complex state of mind—the awareness of an unattainable perfection and, at the same time, of an imperfection too readily attained. "Pleasure and pain combined,"[55] says Baudelaire. And, in this concomitant contemplation of two mutually exclusive worlds, the poet could end up depleting all resources left him if it were not for the recourse he has from the melancholy that preys upon him. It is a recourse he embraces all the more passionately because, contrary to what has often been said, he is not one to surrender easily. Poet of the irremediable, Baudelaire is also, so to speak, the one who says, "Everything is reparable."[56] For him, hope is not only the opposite of despair; it is the other side of the same emotional coin. In order to move from one to the other of these two feelings, one may merely have to turn one over and the other will appear. "Bringing about a creation through the pure logic of opposites,"[57] Baudelaire writes somewhere. Elsewhere he says, "I would counter a blasphemy with heavenward transports, and an obscenity with platonic flowers."[58] To grasp the substance of this last statement one must realize that, in Baudelaire's view, a movement toward heaven springs from blasphemy, and real platonic flowers grow in the midst of obscenity. Thus the fall from grace that marks existence is not without recourse, the latter paradoxically dependent upon the very action by which an existence consummates its downfall. Just as there is antireligion (that is, religion inverted), so too there is a movement of recovery by which antireligion is put right side up. If I believe in the devil, I already believe in God. This is the religion—first practiced invertedly, then restored to its proper position—that Baudelaire puts to use in *Les Fleurs du mal*. "To

53. "Fusées," 1255.   54. "Notes nouvelles sur Edgar Poe."
55. "Salon de 1846," 901.   56. "Hygiène," 1268.
57. "Fragments," 516.   58. "Notes et documents pour son avocat," 181.

extract beauty from evil,"[59] to use his expression, is to transfer the beauty of evil onto good. A rescue operation in extremis; an act not of madness but of reason pushed to its farthest entrenchments; finally, a conviction that antipodal realities attract and ultimately coincide.

We should not be surprised, therefore, if the pleas to which Baudelaire has recourse are often couched in identical terms, even if addressed to apparently incompatible individuals. Hence the admirable couplet:

> Have pity, You alone whom I adore
> From down this black pit where my heart is sped.
>
> *J'implore ta pitié, Toi, l'unique que j'aime,*
> *Du fond du gouffre obscur où mon cœur est tombé.*[60]

To whom is this couplet addressed? To a benevolent or malevolent being? Or similarly, the following line—

> Be blessed, oh my God, who givest suffering,
> *Soyez béni, mon Dieu, qui donnez la souffrance,*[61]

—differs in no way in either tone or sentiment from this:

> O Satan, take pity on my long-endured pain!
> *O Satan, prends pitié de ma longue misère!*[62]

If, as Baudelaire says, prayer is a "reservoir of strength," then that strength can be directed with near equal force in any direction. Black and white magic are but one and the same. Baudelaire rarely distinguishes between them: "There is a magical process at work in prayer." That alone matters, and not the figure invoked. God or Satan, good or evil principle, in Baudelaire there is frequently the awareness of a supernatural presence whose beneficial action, arresting the course of destiny, confers upon the beneficiary a way of feeling and thinking, an "état d'âme" utterly

59. "Projects de préface aux Fleurs du mal," 185.
60. "De profundis clamavi," 31 (40, Desmond Harmsworth).
61. "Bénédiction," 9 (9, David Paul).   62. "Les Litanies de Satan," 116.

different from the one his situation as a fallen being had imposed upon him. Thus there can be no doubt that this intervention, one that Baudelaire repeatedly implores throughout his life, plays a role analogous to that of grace in Christian theology.

Nevertheless, these two forms of grace should not be altogether equated. Christian grace is essentially redemptive. Its goal is to return to man the means of attaining salvation. The grace Baudelaire implores (and at times receives) is of a different sort. It leads him back to what theologians call the state of purity; that is, of man before the Fall. The effective magic of Baudelairean grace is that it takes away the spots from the soul it attains, thus granting it the countenance and feelings of an angel. "I prefer to consider this abnormal state of the mind," Baudelaire writes "as true grace, like a magical mirror in which man is invited to see himself as beautiful; that is, as he should and could be: a type of angelic excitement."[63]

What is essential to Baudelaire's mind is that this state should manifest itself to him as utterly gratuitous; that is, undetermined by any previous state. Thus he escapes, at least temporarily, the concatenation of events constituting his fate. "The wonderful state in which the mind of man is thrown at times, as if by a special grace."[64] In contrast to daily life and to the state of mind it engenders, there is a diametrically opposed state of mind in which, abruptly and without warning or tangible explanation, genius unfolds into grace and happiness. The very gratuitousness itself of what is experienced becomes the guarantor of its authenticity. Whether felicitous chance, divine whim, stroke of luck, or the loss of a jinx, the experience of this happiness is in some way its own proof of being. Consequently, the primary means by which the Baudelairean dream structures itself is by remaining open and available, in order to glean maximum profit from the "visitation" that comes to rescue and inspire the poet.

Baudelaire could have no doubt been content with that—that is to say, could have remained in anticipation of fortuitous events capable not of changing his life but of adorning by their appearance certain favored moments. But he is not of a nature to be

---

63. "Les Paradis artificiels," 348.   64. Ibid, 386.

content with merely temporary modifications. It is not enough for him to feel momentarily redeemed. His existence must be transformed over the entire span of its duration. A life utterly impure, corrupted to its very core, can only be ransomed if the efficacy of grace wholly purifies it. What Baudelaire passionately longed for was not merely, like Banville, a cluster of "heures heureuses" but a sustained existence of felicity, a permanent state of happiness. Nothing is more typical of him than the "dream of eternity," its object to replace time, with its tragic persistance, with an exactly opposite type of duration, which would unfailingly make an entire life flow in a consistent paradisiac state. Incapable of being satisfied with the rare and intermittant visitations of grace, he was thus forced to seek other means of attaining the terrestrial eternity which he coveted.

It is striking that in two different texts, Baudelaire opposes the concept of effort to that of grace.

In his "Notes nouvelles sur Edgar Poe" he writes:

> Poe exerted considerable effort to subjugate to his will the fleeting demon of happy minutes, to remember when he wished those exquisite sensations, those spiritual appreciations, those states of poetic health— so rare and so precious that one could truly see them as moments of grace, as visitations beyond the purview of man.[65]

In a prose poem, "Les Dons des fées," the same opposition occurs, but with greater emphasis:

> What was peculiar, was that the gifts [of the fairies] were not the reward for an effort, but on the contrary, a grace granted to one who had not yet lived.[66]

If we invert this latter text, we have a fairly good grasp of what for Baudelaire is the ideal stance to maintain toward happiness: happiness is something like a gift, but, rather than being granted to one who has not yet lived, it is a reward for effort.

Indeed, Baudelaire is much less a poet of grace than of human effort—doubtless not of completed effort, the result of concen-

65. "Notes nouvelles sur Edgar Poe," 17.   66. "Les Dons des fées," 257.

trated will, but rather of imagined effort, of will construed as a magical means of transformation:

> As architect, it tempted me
> To tame the ocean at its source;
> And this I did,—I made the sea
> Under a jeweled culvert course.

> *Architecte de mes féeries,*
> *Je faisais, à ma volonté,*
> *Sous un tunnel de pierreries*
> *Passer un océan dompté.*[67]

"We have regenerated our soul," says Baudelaire, "by consistent work and contemplation; by the assiduous excercise of the will and the permanent nobility of intention, we have succeeded in creating a garden of true beauty for our use."[68]

Through work, concentration, and the daily excercise of will, it is possible to substitute the fallen being one is with an idealized version, purged of the self. Just as there is an "excercise for strengthening the will,"[69] there are means of instilling one's dreams with the tangible quality of things in the realm of the senses. In other words, there are methodical procedures for remedying the imperfection of what is real. One of these procedures is mnemotechny. Baudelaire, as we have seen, was besieged by all forms of unhappy memory. But he was also haunted by happy memories: joys experienced in the past and one day resuscitated by interpreters such as the sound of a bell or a perfume. These are moments of happiness, triggered by the spreading out of a shock of hair or from the acts of caressing and breathing in the aromas of a body, that unfold in the memory like a vast interior space composed of happy shores, azure skies and distant oases. Now, all this dilation of a remembered life is no longer, in most of these cases, a fortuitous grace; it is rather the result of an art, of a voluntary act:

> I can recall those happy days forgot,
> And see, with head bowed on your knees, my past.

---

67. *Tableau parisien*, "Rêve parisien," 98 (130, Edna St. Vincent Millay).
68. "Les Paradis artificiels," 387.   69. "Le Peintre de la vie moderne," 1139.

27

Je sais l'art d'évoquer les minutes heureuses
Et revis mon passé blotti dans tes genoux.[70]

And if the hair of the beloved emerges with its perfume from a multitude of memories, it is again through a purposeful act of will. "I *want* to shake it in the air like a handkerchief!"[71] says the lover. Poetry and the poetic state, which is both its mainspring and its consequence, are thus not born of chance. By means of a deliberate movement of thought, the mind succeeds in establishing itself, as if forever, in the most fertile hours of existence. These alone are worthy of being preserved or relived. Art is an evocative sorcery, a mnemotechny of the beautiful. This is most particularly manifest in painting, namely in that of Eugène Delacroix: "Painting arises above all from the memory, speaks above all to the memory."[72] "The work of Delacroix," Baudelaire writes elsewhere, "at times appears as a type of mnemotechny of man's grandeur and native passion."[73] Equally mnemonic to Baudelaire are the works of Boudin, Manet, and several others whose innovative painting he was to discover at the end of his life. For, contrary to what is often believed, the exclusive goal of impressionism is not to capture immediate impressions; it functions, rather, as a memory aid in various forms to bring forth in one time period the impressions felt in another. "If they [the spectators] had seen, as I did recently in M. Boudin's studio . . . several hundred pastel studies, improvised in front of the sea and sky, they would then have understood . . . the gulf that separates a study from a picture . . . M. Boudin knows quite well that all this will have to be turned into a picture, by means of the poetic impression recalled at will."[74]

Here we have the essential point. Painting, poetry, all forms of art, are but a means by which to remember at will certain states of sensibility and of the intellect. Genius itself, no matter what its manifestation, "is but childhood recovered at will,"[75] that is, a mnemonic power both adjustable and tractable, at the mercy of whoever uses it, for the purpose of forcing a certain number of perceptible materials, stored up during childhood, to reappear in

70. "Le Balcon," 35 (46, F. P. Sturm).   71. "La Chevelure," 25.
72. "Salon de 1846," 891.   73. "L'Oeuvre et la vie de Delacroix," 1117.
74. "Salon de 1859," 1082.   75. "Le Peintre et la vie moderne," 1159.

the mind and, consequently, in the work produced as well. This holds true for both the poet and the painter. For example, Edgar Poe (in the manner of Delacroix, according to Baudelaire), subjects his memory to "the fugitive demon of happy minutes"[76] and asserts that "only he who is master of his memory is a poet."[77]

It becomes clear then that Baudelaire's mnemotechny (despite various similarities to Proust, which Proust himself labels a precursor's project) differs greatly from the Proustian method. For if we agree that the Proustian memory is, like the Baudelairean, the rediscovery of a childhood impression, in Proust's view it is futile to hope to resuscitate this impression *at will*. And this is because truly voluntary memories, devoid of strength and freshness, are neither efficacious nor usable. Baudelaire's position is entirely different. For him, the involuntary memory has the flaw of being accidental. What the poet *wants* is a memory that remains perpetually at the artist's disposal, which he can use when he chooses to restore the feelings which had once been his.

Contrary to Proust, then, Baudelaire disregards the role of forgetting, of erosion—distractions, omissions, and platitudes that often have such a fatal effect upon memory. For him, memory remains intact and, if well protected, generally preserves its regenerative power. Herein lies the great contrast with Proust. The latter has a well-defined goal, which consists in attaining an atemporal essence through the intermediary of memory. What fundamentally matters for him is neither the past nor the present impression but, rather, that which they have in common. Baudelaire demands something very different of the mnemonic experience. What he wishes to obtain from it is the annihilation of his state as a fallen being, and his permanent induction into a state of unchanging happiness. For him, mnemotechny is a means of "disturbing one's destiny in order to put a new type of fate in its place"—a fate that might generate happiness and with the specific role of substituting itself for the baleful destiny of the fallen being.

Thus the cult that Baudelaire dedicates to childhood must be understood in this very specific sense. The child is not an angel.

76. "Notes nouvelles sur Edgar Poe."   77. Ibid.

Still in close proximity to the Fall, he is a barbarian, as dangerous as he is wicked. But he possesses an essential gift; one the adult can neither rediscover nor appropriate: the gift of childish perception. "The child sees everything as novel; he is always intoxicated. No aspect of life is dull to him."[78] In short, there is in the childish vision of the world, "a compulsory idealization, resulting from . . . a sharpened perception, magical by its simplicity."[79]

Either by recapturing his former powers, now lost, or by belatedly plumbing the fund of ingenuous impressions he has accumulated, the adult is capable in certain circumstances of experiencing the "exaltation of the senses and the mind."

> There are days when man awakens with a young and energetic genius. His eyelids barely rid of the sleep that had sealed them, man sees the external world offer itself to him in a prominent relief, a sharpness of contour, and a wealth of awesome colors.[80]

In this extremely important text, the magical acuity of perception manifests itself in two ways: in the sharpness of contour and in the intensity of color. The outlines project themselves, the colors penetrate the mind "with victorious intensity." In a word, "the more sensitive senses perceive more resounding sensations."[81] Moreover, the genius of imaginative powers corresponds to the intensity of sensation. The inventiveness of the imagination is added to the perception of reality. A magical transformation of both external nature and the spectator's nature is thus magically achieved.

All of Baudelairean thought is, as we have seen, based upon an opposition between what is natural (fallen) and supernatural (dreamed). The imagination provides the means for overcoming this opposition. Suddenly nature coincides with the world of dreams. Suddenly the creature one is, delivered of its physical and moral ugliness, begins to resemble the being one has dreamed of becoming. And this dual transformation is by no means born of chance, of some type of divine or demonic grace, but,

---

78. "Le Peintre de la vie moderne," 1159.   79. Ibid., 1162.
80. "Les Paradis artificiels," 347.   81. "Exposition universelle de 1855," 974.

rather, of the very act of the subject, who, in using his imagination, extracts a paradise from a hell and a flower of beauty from the evil in which he is constrained to live.

What is most magical about the imagination's activity is the veneer of supernatural interest with which it covers a world both interior and exterior, a world hitherto condemned to manifest the gloomiest appearance. "The magical glaze that extends over all of life," that "colors it in solemnity and illuminates it in all its profundity."

In illuminating existence in all its depth, the veneer of the imagination once again gives the Baudelairean view of life this additional dimension (already noted in the previous chapter), a kind of vast, inner spaciousness. What a transformation is created by the magic of the imagination! In the eyes of the individual who is conscious of universal perversion, nature is a narrow vault, closed off by a ceiling. And it is only at the other side of this ceiling that free space begins. By using the imagination, however, the universe unlocks. It becomes an "immense profundity," gaily tilled by the mind. The most intoxicating experience for Baudelaire is a dream in which he feels himself to be flying, swimming, floating in a vast expanse. The greatest of Baudelairean dreams are those of expansion; dreams in which it seems that, in order better to harmonize with the infinite power of dilation that the human mind can achieve, the expanse unfolds, leaving thought free to maneuver without obstacle. But these are also dreams in which thought seems to expand and, even more, to grasp itself in the act by which it takes possession of space. It is often an act of multiplication. This act of taking hold of nature supernaturalized is then accomplished in a guise that is in fact quantitative, by means of an enraptured proliferation of numbers. Following a resemblance analogous to the creative act itself, engendering the universe in the form of a "population of innumerable numerals" (later to inspire Rimbaud), the poet becomes aware of the multitude of distinctly particular entities that constitute creation. As a result, the perception of what is tends to become something comparable to a colossal "arithmetical operation in which numbers engender numbers,"[82] as occurs at times when one listens to music while under the influence of hashish.

82. "Les Paradis artificiels," 365.

Of all the French poets, Baudelaire is perhaps the one with the most developed intuition for sensing the numerical dynamism that endlessly manifests itself in the tiniest of movements. Number is a translation of space,"[83] says Baudelaire. It is a numbered space, which grows indefinitely by dint of the movement at play within it. Number swells space and pushes it to explosion.

Nevertheless, the movement of multiplication under discussion here cannot be truly apprehended by an immobile spectator. It is only by accompanying the moving body in its trajectory that thought can grasp movement in all of its plenitude. Baudelaire excels in describing the displacement of the object, as if he himself were moving from his place:

> The sea your mirror, you look into your mind
> In its eternal billows surging without end.

> *La mer est ton miroir; tu contemples ton âme*
> *Dans le déroulement infini de sa lame.*[84]

In a text such as this, the stated analogy between the sea and the human soul suggests a movement simultaneously perceived from the outside and experienced from the inside. It is a motion whose particularity lies in its ability to preserve itself, as is, across space, which is its essence. The same holds true for the bodily movement in the following two texts. The first of the two has to do with the movement of the female body as it is perceived by the spectator:

> As the long weeds that float among the surge,
> She folds indifference round her budding life.

> *Comme les longs réseaux de la houle des mers*
> *Elle se développe avec indifférence.*[85]

In the second text the movement is the lover's caress, as it follows the contours of the beloved's body:

> For fervently I would have rained, my Sweet,
> Fond kisses over all thy form divine
> Even from thy black tresses to thy feet . . .

83. "Mon cœur mis à nu," 1296.
84. "L'Homme et la mer," 18 (21, Ruthven Todd).
85. 27 (36, F. P. Sturm).

Car j'eusse avec ferveur baisé ton noble corps,
Et depuis tes pieds nus jusqu'à tes noires tresses
Déroulé le trésor des profondes caresses.[86]

At times the movement is simply retraced as it appears to the eye, beginning in the place where, taking flight, it starts to unfold. This is how, in Baudelaire, we often witness the rising tide, metaphorical or real.

Yet sadness rises in me like the sea . . .

Whence, did you say, does this strange sadness rise,
Like tides that over naked black rocks flow?

Smiling in triumph from the heights of her couch
At my desire advancing, as gentle and deep
As the sea sending its waves to the warm beach.

Mais la tristesse en moi monte comme la mer.[87]

D'où vous vient, disiez-vous, cette tristesse étrange,
Montant comme la mer sur le roc noir et nu?[88]

Et du haut du divan elle souriait d'aise
A mon amour profond et doux comme la mer,
Qui vers elle montait comme vers sa falaise.[89]

In this association between feeling and the movement of the sea, a vast, collective impetus can be distinguished, shaping itself and rising; an emotional tide or the swelling wave, ready to gather itself into a wide undulation. Similarly, for Baudelaire there are privileged places from which a movement may be discerned, destined to expand from there into space. Such are the harbors [*ports*], from which ships can be seen trimming their sails "for a distant sky."

Here again the female body is presented to us in its cinematic analogy with the sea and the objects floating upon it:

And on the salt waves of your grief
My longings swollen with hope shall ride,
Like a ship that puts to sea.

86. "Une nuit que j'étais . . ." 32 (43, Sir John Squire).
87. "Causerie," 54 (71, Sir John Squire).
88. "Semper eadem," 39 (51, Peter Hellings).
89. "Les Bijoux," 142 (27, David Paul).

> *Mon désir gonflé d'espérance*
> *Sur tes pleurs salés nagera*
> *Comme un vaisseau qui prend le large.*[90]

And this next passage, more *developed*, charged with rippling poetry, like the very object it describes:

> When you go sweeping your wide skirts, to me
> You seem a splendid ship that out to sea
>   Spreads its full sails, and with them
> Goes rolling in a soft, slow, lazy rhythm.

> *Quand tu vas balayant l'air de ta jupe large,*
> *Tu fais l'effet d'un beau vaisseau qui prend le large,*
>   *Chargé de toile, et va roulant*
> *Suivant un rythme doux, et paresseux, et lent.*[91]

The magic of movement in Baudelaire has the peculiar ability to reconstitute itself in the verbal image given it by the poet, thus offering the reader a rhetorical version of exact equivalence, as if physical space corresponded to that occupied by words, and the dynamism of the poem took place in this new expanse with the same nonchalance as a ship or a woman walking. One of the forms of movement in the reproduction of which Baudelaire excels is movement of the utmost slowness. Not that this indolent slowness need be confused with the tragic slowing down, the gradual paralysis of every effort, of which we spoke in the previous chapter. Here existence does not slide toward a total immobility, the metaphorical shape of nothingness. Each time the movement seems to be on the verge of expiring, it begins anew with the same softness, but in a different direction. Such is the case with the rocking motion, always linked in Baudelaire's mind to the concept of rhythm and softness:

> My subtle spirit then will know a measure
> Of fertile idleness and fragrant leisure,
> Lulled by the infinite rhythm of its tides!

> *Et mon esprit subtil que le roulis caresse*
> *Saura vous retrouver, ô féconde paresse,*
> *Infinis bercements du loisir embaumé!*[92]

90. "L'Héautontimorouménos," 74 (97, Naomi Lewis).
91. "Le Beau Navire," 49 (66, Roy Campbell).
92. "La Chevelure," 25 (32, Doreen Bell).

"The happiness that the rocking motion brings, celebrated by Baudelaire in unforgottable tones," writes Jean-Pierre Richard, "is based on its calm, its harmony, its deep affinity with the individual who welcomes it within himself. Its back and forth motion balances and swings life around a steady axis."[93] There is both a duality and a complexity in Baudelaire's rocking motion. The mobility of the back and forth motion is allied and opposed to the steadiness of the axis. The former, moreover, suggests less movement than a succession thereof, obeying the same generating principle. Herein lies all the importance of *rhythm* in Baudelaire's poetry, for rhythm is essentially a steady multiplicity of movements which harmonize in their succession. At the heart of rhythm, even if it cannot be clearly discerned as such, there is always and above all an *undulation:*

> Who among us has not dreamt of a particular and poetical prose for translating the lyrical movements of the mind, the undulations of reverie and the quiverings of consciousness?[94]

In order to come into being, this lyricism of undulation must always have a multiplicity of elements captured in a movement which coordinates them. Thus the movement of the female body, with its clothing and adornments, is compared by Baudelaire to "an undulating instrument, glittering and perfumed."[95] Revealed here is all the multiplicity of the feminine world in its gait both fluid [*fondue*] and multifarious [*nombreuse*]. For Baudelaire, then, the sentence and image contain not only a rhythm but a combination of harmonized rhythmic parts as well. This is what he calls *eurhythmy*. He writes: "Harmony, the balancing motion of the lines, and eurhythmy in the movements appear to the dreamer as necessities, as compulsions—not only for all living beings in creation, but for him, the dreamer, who at this point in his crisis finds himself to be gifted with a miraculous capacity for understanding immortal and universal rhythm."[96]

In this particular case, let us not attach too much importance to the fact that the magic of eurhythmic movement is caused by the

---

93. Jean-Pierre Richard, *Poésie et profondeur* (Paris: Seuil, 1955), 142.
94. "Projets et plans," 311.   95. "Les Paradis artificiels," 445.
96. Ibid, 377.

use of stimulants. Whether Baudelaire's paradises are obtained by the intervention of creative free will or by the contrivance of drugs, the result is the same; the happy revelation of universal harmony in movement; a movement which, as we have said, is both *multiple* and *one, continuous* and *varied.* Whether it be woman, frigate, or complex feeling, a collective reality displaces itself in external space or in thought, in the form of a synthesis of elements which are always balancing and always combined. It is like a structure consisting of distinct and isolable parts, but doubly joined by natural affinities and by a certain similarity of movement. Few images are as delectable to the Baudelairean imagination as these shapes both multiple and mobile, permitting the eye to move between facets and perspectives, thus seeing them endlessly renewing themselves without once diverging from their obedience to an ordering principle which rules over them and maintains their cohesion in motion. So it is that the clouds in the sky, as well as the dreams in the mind, appear to Baudelaire in the characteristic form of a *mobile architecture:*

> Through the open window of the dining room, I contemplated the moving architectures that God creates with vapor, marvelous constructions of the impalpable.[97]

> Awesome and monstrous architectures arose in his mind, like those moving constructions that the eye of the poet perceives in clouds colored by the setting sun.

This particular mobility, here joined to the appearance (usually rigorously static) of architectural forms, is perhaps most evident in those places subjected to the vacillations of water and light: harbors.

> A harbor provides a lovely rest for a soul exhausted by life's struggles. The fullness of the sky, the mobile architecture of the clouds, the changing colors of the sea, the twinkling of the beacons—all are a prism, marvelously constructed to amuse the eyes without ever boring them.[98]

97. "La Soupe et les nuages," 298.   98. "Le Port," 292.

Baudelaire's affection for harbors is to be found again in his appreciation of the female body, it too being a mobile architecture. "He appreciated a beautiful body," says Baudelaire of Samuel Cramer, his prototype. "It was like a material harmony, like beautiful architecture complete with motion."[99]

Architecture, complete with motion! Order in variety and variety in order! Baudelairean thought revels in these harmonic opposites. It especially revels in the works of Delacroix. What is to be found in these? The same that is to be found in the displays of nature—that is, says Baudelaire, an infinite series of curved, receding and broken lines, "which conform to a law of flawless generation, where parallelism is always indecisive and sinuous, where the concave and the convex mirror and pursue each other."[100]

The sinuous lines in Delacroix's paintings are therefore—like the lines in nature—also a mobile architecture. It is an architecture which at first glance appears to be concealed by the profusion of perspectives and the multiplicity of forms. This is because the latter, in contrast to the stability of the central motif, constitute a variety of successive angles, a variety which is of temporal essence. Thus it is not unreasonable to maintain that any Delacroix painting is at once a spatial unfolding and a temporal development. In this way, time develops and enriches space.

This becomes particularly clear in a natural phenomenon which, more than any other, attracted Baudelaire's attention: the phenomenon of light. The marvelous passage he placed at the beginning of the third chapter to his *Salon de 1846* is well known. In it, he dedicates a veritable hymn to color:

> Let us suppose a beautiful expanse of nature, where everything is at liberty to be as green, red, dusty or iridescent as it wishes; where all things, variously colored in accordance with their molecular structure, undergo continual alteration through the transposition of shadow and light; where the workings of latent heat vibrate ceaselessly, causing lines to tremble and fulfilling the law of eternal and universal movement.[101]

99. "La Fanfarlo," 509.   100. "Exposition universelle de 1855," 973.
101. "Salon de 1846," 880.

The passage is too familiar to warrant being cited in its entirety. Let us remember only that, for Baudelaire, color is endowed with the same power of mobility as line; it possesses the same undulation and the same means of infinite variety. In the rest of the passage, the impression of mobility is further strengthened by the awareness of the changing hours, minutes, and seconds. An inexhaustible series of nuances follow one another, their hues continuously altered by the changes in light, "multiplying their melodious unions to infinity." This comparison of *mobile color* to music seems in fact particularly pleasing to Baudelaire. Several lines later, in the same text, he refers to it as a symphony, a "succession of melodies whose variety ever issues from the infinite," forming a "complex hymn" that is called color.

When thus perceived by Baudelaire, time, with its generative movement diversified in the multitude of its sequential manifestations, indeed becomes an enrichment of space. Through the nearly imperceptible modulations that time engenders, space becomes ornamented, more complex and more apt to put its mass of properties into relief. Once again, we find ourselves in the presence of what we may term Baudelaire's mathematical genius, his ability to grasp reality in its multiplicity. But it is no longer the perception of a simple numerical reality that is at issue here nor, consequently, that of an arithmetical poetry. Baudelaire, perceiving space and time in the multiplicity of relations there engendered, juxtaposes to his arithmetic genius a perfectly geometric one. This becomes evident in another well-known passage from *Fusée;* a passage which, because of its importance, will be cited nearly in its entirety. Once again, there is a ship, and perhaps as well, a woman walking:

> I believe that the endless and mysterious charm that lies in the contemplation of a ship, especially a moving ship, comes first from regularity and symmetry, which are among the primordial necessities of the human spirit (at the same level as complexity and harmony), and, second, from the successive multiplication and the generation of all the curves and imaginary figures brought about in space by the real elements of the object.
>
> The poetic idea that emerges from this process of motion within lines is the hypothesis of an immense

being; a being complicated but eurhythmic, a creature full of genius, suffering and sighing over all sighs and all human ambitions.[102]

This interior space, the one into which the poet's thought projects itself, enjoys the same properties as external space. It has its depth, complexity and eurhythmy. An entire generation of curves and of figures, "constantly varying their play,"[103] stretches out into the expanse of mental life as it does into the expanse outside.

Baudelaire, then, is not only the explorer of human depth and spatial immensities; he is also the discoverer of the "complications" which branch out from them. And this second discovery has something so fascinating about it and unveils such a wealth of riches that Baudelaire is often tempted to concentrate his attention exclusively on this single aspect of things. It is this discovery that seems to him, if not the most magical among them all, at least the most abundant, the most multifarious, and the one that seizes the artist's imagination most directly. The latter, he says of Constantin Guys, is "as if overwhelmed by a mass of details, all of which demand justice, with the fury of a crowd in love with absolute equality."[104]

This abundance is comparable to the excessive growth of rampant vegetation. Baudelaire willingly abandons himself to the ecstatic intoxication imparted by "the arabesque of sounds"[105] and the "sinuosity of lines."[106] He takes passionate pleasure in "the beauty of the multicolored and the variegated that moves in the infinite spirals of life."[107] "It is an immense joy to take up residence within the undulating, within movement, within the fleeting and the infinite."[108] And yet, in Baudelaire, consciousness of movement is not solely the awareness of the mass of coordinates to which movement gives birth at any given point in its trajectory. The complexity of the real is neither mad nor anar-

102. "Fusées," 1261.   103. "Conseils aux jeunes littérateurs," 478.
104. "Le Peintre de la vie moderne," 1167.
105. "Richard Wagner et Tannhäuser," 1219.
106. "Les Paradis artificiels," 375.
107. "Exposition universelle de 1855," 955.
108. "Le Peintre de la vie moderne," 1160.

chical. It is governed by a principle as important as the power of variation and proliferation. Consequently, Baudelaire is brought to consider movement from the same dualistic perspective that he takes for all his other experiences. Movement is *dual*. It is both the rectilinear surge toward a point of arrival, and the collection of interlacings which, in their meandering paths, surround this fixed surge. This is not to say that Baudelaire accepts the superiority of the straight line. For example, Cramer, his hero, "profoundly hated" (and, adds Baudelaire, "in my opinion he was perfectly right") those long straight lines of apartment buildings and the architecture imported into private homes."[109] Similarly, Baudelaire detests the works of Ingres and his disciples because he believes he discerns in them the oppression of the curved line by the straight. On the other hand, he praises Delacroix for not allowing the system of straight lines to invade his originality. "The people in his works are always moving and the draperies always flying about."[110] Delacroix's painting, however, does not fall prey to a mere swarming of activity, any more than does the poetry of Baudelaire. In both, two principles are put into action simultaneously: rectilinearity and imaginative exuberance. They tend to converge. Baudelaire, influenced by De Quincey, conceives of the union of straight and curved lines as a symbolic manifestation of a thyrse, or a caduceus. "De Quincey," he says, "at one point compares his thought to a thyrse, that simple rod that gains all of its charm from the complicated foliage surrounding it."[111] The passage in which De Quincey refers to the thyrse appears in none of the editions of the *Confessions*. It is to be found only in the first version of the *Suspiria*, which was published in the *Blackwood Magazine*. Here is the essential section:

> The whole course of this narrative resembles, and was meant to resemble, a *caduceus* wreathed about with meandering ornaments, or the shaft of a tree's stem hung round and surmounted with some vagrant parasitical plant . . . The true object in my "Opium Confessions" is not the naked physiological theme . . . but those wandering musical variations upon the theme—those parasitical thoughts, feelings, digres-

109. "La Fanfarlo," 508.   110. "Salon de 1846," 892.
111. "Les Paradis artificiels," 390.

sions, which climb up with bells and blossoms round about the arid stock; ramble away from it at times with perhaps too rank a luxuriance; but at the same time, by the eternal interest attached to the *subjects* of these digressions, no matter what were the execution, spread a glory over incidents that for themselves would be—less than nothing.[112]

Baudelaire summarizes this passage by De Quincey as follows:

The subject has no more value than a dry, bare stick. But the ribbons, the vines, and the flowers can provide, by their playful intertwinings, a wealth of treasures for the eye.

And Baudelaire adds:

The thought of De Quincey is not merely sinuous— that word does not convey sufficient strength-; it is a natural spiralling.[113]

Baudelaire's thought is no less spiraled: it is digressive and yet arched toward its goal, somehow wrapping its imaginative movement around the impetus which carries it forward. It is a caduceus thought, to use De Quincey's words or, to use those of Baudelaire, a thyrse thought. One is reminded of the prose poem Baudelaire dedicates to this capricious emblematic structure:

What is a thyrse? . . . a staff . . . Around this staff, in capricious meanderings, stalks and flowers frolic and play, the latter sinuous and fleeting, the former bowed like bells or overturned chalices. And an astonishing radiance emanates from this *complexity of lines*. Do not the arched and spiraled lines appear to be wooing the straight one and dancing around it in mute ador-ation?[114]

In the preceding sentences, Baudelaire does no more than follow (indeed, with obvious pleasure, and with several added flourishes) the image conceived by De Quincey. But now he adds

112. "Suspiria de profundis," *Blackwood's Edinburgh Magazine*, 58, no. 303 (March 1845): 273.
113. "Les Paradis artificiels," 461.   114. "Le Thyrse," 285.

to this fragment an amplification which is nowhere to be found in his mentor and which is the very precise expression of Baudelaire's own thought. Once again, it is a dualistic thought in which the opposition between the straight and curved becomes that between rigor of thought and imaginative fancy:

> The thyrse is the representation of your surprising duality . . . The staff is your will: straight, firm, and steadfast. The flowers are the strollings of your fancy around your will; it is the feminine aspect performing wondrous pirouettes around the male. Straight line and line of arabesques, intention and expression, inflexibility of the will, sinuosity of the verb, unity of the goal, variety of means, all-powerful and indivisible amalgam of genius—what artist could possess the loathsome courage to divide and separate you?[115]

What artist will have the capacity to grasp in its complexity that which is at once a duality of creative thought and a duality of the object it represents? The thyrse is simultaneously will and caprice, but also unity and multiplicity. As we have already noted, the world of Baudelaire reveals itself from the double perspective of depth and complexity. At times, as with the thyrse, this dual perspective is represented by the poet in the form of the earliest movement, simple and direct, that leads the mind toward the depth of being. At the same time, however, another movement unites with space by means of all the ramifications of its coordinates. But at yet other times this double quality of space is manifest in another kind of association of opposites: in the unity and the contrast, in many representations of spatial expanse, created by the multiplication of lines in the foreground and simplicity in the background. This remains to be examined in order to understand the act by which the Baudelairean imagination, in taking possession of the space which surrounds it, is able to supernaturalize it.

Indeed, Baudelaire's work often describes another kind of movement—that of a moving object against a motionless background. This movement is expressed in various ways: strange fanfares glide under a sky of gloom; a rising tide splashes over a black boulder. Hearses file down city streets, the image of a

115. Ibid.

splenetic soul. Monuments emerge from a deep expanse. Once again, then, the visions of hashish spread their hues, their shudders, and their light over the whole of existence, revealing its depth.

No matter what metaphorical or real movement is here suggested by the poet, the unmoving background element from which the moving object detaches itself is almost invariably represented in the form of a dark expanse. In the poem "Le Chat" there is a "pearly and filtered" voice that lies, writes Baudelaire, "in the darkest of my depths."[116] In another poem, "Confession," memory emerges "against the dark depths of my soul."[117] On the one hand, there is the surge or current of thought emanating from the mind; on the other hand, there is this same mind, depicted as a somber depth, creating a contrast with the moving luminosity of mental life.

Is this not also true of the famous invocation to Death in "Le Voyage"?

> It's time. Old Captain, lift anchor, sink!
> The land rots; we shall sail into the night;
> if now the sky and sea are black as ink
> our hearts, as you must know, are filled with light.
>
> *O Mort, vieux capitaine, il est temps, levons l'ancre!*
> *Ce pays nous ennuie, ô Mort!: appareillons!*
> *Si le ciel et la mer sont noirs comme de l'encre,*
> *Nos cœurs que tu connais sont remplis de rayons.*[118]

The radiance of emotion is here opposed to the gloomy monotony of external space. A cluster of lights projects itself onto a dark background. The light depends upon the background, without which it could not be distinguished and might never reach us. For Baudelaire, then, all affirmation of movement, of life and of light frequently tends to be coupled with, to depend upon, an inverse reality—a negative one, devoid of movement, life, and light, providing it with the background:

> An artist God has set apart
> In mockery, I paint the murk.

116. "Le Chat," 48.   117. "Confession," 43.
118. "Le Voyage," 127 (185, Robert Lowell).

Je suis comme un peintre qu'un Dieu moqueur
Condamne à peindre, hélas! sur les ténèbres.[119]

Antoine Adam is correct in comparing these words with De Quincey's comment that many children, maybe most, have the ability to paint, so to speak, all kinds of phantoms onto shadows. Baudelaire expanded this remark in "Les Paradis artificiels": "Children are generally endowed with the singular ability to perceive, or rather create, on the fertile canvas of darkness, an entire world of strange visions."[120]

But children are not alone in their ability to cast the variegated quality of their visions upon the screen of an existence in itself fundamentally somber: the poet is a painter who paints upon a background of night; and the musician is as well. Poe moves his phosphorescent figures upon purplish and greenish backgrounds; and Wagner, with his fiery and despotic music, "paints upon a backdrop of darkness, torn by reverie, the vertiginous designs of opium."[121]

Finally, referring to himself, Baudelaire says:

At night I watch God's knowing finger trace
Unending nightmares on the dark unending.

Sur le fond de mes nuits Dieu de son doigt savant
Dessine un cauchemar multiforme et sans trêve.[122]

Whether the background of the painting be here the poet's thought, on which a divine or infernal will leaves its mark and makes its influence felt, or whether it be something else—the result is the same: in the black chamber of interior life, luminous figures file by, like characters of the magic lantern on a canvas screen. "Darkness is a canvas,"[123] says Baudelaire in the poem "Obsession." No doubt Baudelaire alludes to the play of the magic lantern (so important to Proust's development as well) when he writes:

We want to break the boredom of our jails . . .
give us visions to stretch our minds like sails,
the blue, exotic shoreline of your dream!

119. "Les Ténèbres," 36 (48, Lewis Piaget Shanks).
120. "Les Paradis artificiels," 426.
121. "Richard Wagner et Tannhäuser," 1214.
122. "Le Gouffre," 172 (194, Jackson Mathews).   123. "Obsession," 71.

Faites, pour égayer l'ennui de nos prisons,
Passer sur nos esprits tendus comme une toile
Vos souvenirs avec leurs cadres d'horizon.[124]

Thus there are two distinct aspects and, one might say, two levels making up the life of the mind. There is a first state, comparable to a space of shades, of which nothing, it would seem, can shatter the monotony. But there is also, rupturing the uniformity of that surface, a parade of images, mostly luminous, which may be the whimsical shapes of the mind or of memories. The duality of blackness and of clarity is produced at times in the form of alternations and at times in that of simultaneity. Most often, however, these two contradictory aspects are entangled, and what remains for us to examine is their fusions.

In Baudelaire, there is a curious reversal to be found in the usual relation between night and light; a reversal indicated by the theme he so often takes up—twilight. On the one hand, as we have seen, twilight is the death agony of light, its slow engulfment into "the vast and black abyss." Day is consumed by "the victorious oppression of night." It is an oppression that effects not only the gradual extinction of the vanquished night but the halting of its correlative—that is, motion. By covering it with a veil, night drowns the sun "in coagulating blood." Barely subsisting are the vestiges of daylight's former animation, the dizzy perfume of the flowers, and the final murmer of diurnal life. The overriding sensation is that of life's slow descent into the abyss, light sliding into night, and the present into the past. Yet the kind of struggle that pits night against day does not end as definitively as one might expect, by the victory of the death principle. For suddenly "the delicious past emerges from under the black present." It is a "luminous past," with a heart that "gathers up all vestiges." The result is that the engulfing night becomes the very medium by which the images which the mind had seen darken or disappear are restored to it. This reappearance of the past in the form of memory is represented on two occasions as the new emergence of light from the bosom of darkness: "memory *shines* like a monstrance," and the stars "light up . . . under the night's deep mourning." In order to describe this return of light through the dark veil that covers it, Baudelaire in a prose poem employs the following admirable metaphor: "One is reminded of . . . one

124. "Le Voyage," 124 (181, Robert Lowell).

of those strange dresses worn by dancers, a dress covered by a transparant and somber gauze, which occasionally allows a fleeting glance at the various splendors of a glittering petticoat.[125]

Thus, twilight is not limited to consummating the triumph of night over day. It also marks a positive relation between initially hostile elements. Whereas in the preceding texts, we had a background of night, out of which luminous figures were carved, here we see a curtain of shades, crisscrossed by flashes of light. At times moving on a backdrop of darkness, at others cauterizing it with tongues of flame, light is always associated with that which veils it, forming a complicated relation with its opposite; one difficult to disentangle.

Is it not the same with moonlight? Like twilight, moonlight is soft, and lacks the hardness of the light of noon. It is, rather, a light bathed in darkness. In a prose poem, Baudelaire describes it invading a certain room and the soul of a certain child. Soundlessly passing through the window panes, stretching itself over the being it touches with a kind of supple tenderness, it spreads itself everywhere "like a phosphoric atmosphere; like a luminous poison."[126] It is a light, but a nocturnal one, a marriage of light and night which, while possessing the illuminating powers of solar light, enjoys the dangerous advantages of the world of darkness.

This surprising union of day and night manifests itself more clearly in another light phenomenon of which Baudelaire dreams: the midnight sun and the aurora borealis. The long, polar twilight delights the poet because "the sun's gaze upon the earth is only oblique," and "the slow alternations between light and night obliterate variety and increase monotony, that other face of nothingness." On the one hand, thought can take "long baths of darkness" here; on the other hand, it is entertained by "the rosy sprays of the aurora borealis," the reflection, says Baudelaire, "of hell's fireworks."[127]

Let us not pause on the diabolical nature of nocturnal light. We have already alluded to it. Let us be content with examining the nonsolar properties of certain lights, and the fact that, diffusing into the night, they appear to emanate from it. Any light that

125. "Le Crépuscule du soir," 263. 126. "Les Bienfaits de la lune," 290.
127. "Anywhere out of the world," 304.

does not originate directly from the sun seems to Baudelaire more beautiful, richer in meaning, because its source is a principle of illumination different from that of daylight. The Baudelairean universe, it has often been noted, is a world more nocturnal than diurnal; a world illuminated by kerosene lamps and street lights, in which even the candle plays a role all the more important because the feeble circle of brightness it casts is circumscribed by a vast circle of darkness.

> No object is more profound, more mysterious, more fertile, more obscure, more dazzling, than a window illuminated by a candle.[128]

In Baudelaire's universe, the glimmer of a flame is often coupled with a certain density of darkness. The two confront and touch each other, dramatically increasing their potency as well by dint of their conjunction. Just as in chiaroscuro compositions, found in the works of certain mannerist painters such as Rembrandt and Delacroix, the Baudelairean imagination reaches its highest satisfaction when the contact between two warring elements has brought them to such a high degree of intimacy that, through an exchange of their opposing properties, each is in the position of being metamorphosed into the other. Then light becomes obscure, and obscurity luminous.

Let us go back to the picture of the naked woman in the poem "Les Bijoux":

> —And the lamp having at last resigned itself to death,
> There was nothing now but firelight in the room,
> And every time a flame uttered a gasp for breath
> It flushed her amber skin with the blood of its bloom.

> —*Et la lampe s'étant résignée à mourir,*
> *Comme le foyer seul illuminait la chambre,*
> *Chaque fois qu'il poussait un flamboyant soupir,*
> *Il inondait de sang cette peau couleur d'ambre!*[129]

At first glance, it would appear that the significance of this scene lies in the general reduction of light. As in the theme of twilight, the gradual weakening of the sources of light consummates the triumph of the forces of night. And yet what remains is

---

128. "Le fenêtres," 288.   129. "Les Bijoux," 142 (27–28, David Paul).

the impression of a transferral. Not without loss, but with a certain persistence, the light continues to shine, displacing its center of activity from one object to another, from the lamp to the hearth, and from the hearth to the body upon which it casts its glow. Now, as this phenomenon occurs, a change seems to take place in the quality of the lighting, such that in decreasing its intensity it simultaneously increases its intimacy, its warmth, its peculiarly human existence—as if its red glow were the sign of a fundamental permutation of fire, whereby it would no longer be impossible to believe in the transformation, from a distance, of embers into a flower of flesh and blood. In this way, our idea is confirmed: that, for Baudelaire, light is never more possessed of a magical power than when it clearly differs from *natural* light, that is, solar light. In one sense, this is no doubt true of all artificial light. The latter, no matter what its form, always appears, to the one for whom it sheds light, somewhat *detached* from the light of day. But in Baudelaire this capacity takes on the guise of an illegal substitution. The moon, a lamp, the hearth, a woman's skin—all are stars of increasingly limited radius, taking upon themselves the normal activities of the star of day. Like Prometheus, they are fire stealers. If the enchanting evening is the criminal's friend, if it comes like a conspirator on soft wolf tread, it is because it is itself undertaking a criminal act. Stealthily it replaces legitimate with stolen light, with a light that illegitimately constitutes itself into an autonomous hearth. This is evident in the poem "Bijoux." Surreptitiously, when all other luminous activity has ceased or nearly ceased, when the lamp has resigned itself to death and the hearth barely utters a few last burning sighs—we see the skin of the naked woman, drenched as it is in the reddish glow, transform itself in turn into a luminous hearth. Thus, without Baudelaire saying so, through the gradual transferral of light sources among themselves, a woman's skin seems finally to become the diffusing center of all light. It transforms itself into an autonomous power of illumination, alchemically created by the metamorphosis of igneus power into blood, and of blood into a luminous flesh.

Now we can more clearly perceive the direction taken by Baudelairean poetry: toward replacing, whenever possible, the single light of day with independant lights, thus introducing into its own universe, in the place of celestial light's simplicity, an indefinite plurality of the sources of light. Baudelaire's universe is one of lamps, chandeliers, streetlights, all types of lighting instruments whose function is to capture, alter, recreate, or reflect light.

Woman, with her skin and jewels, is the most dazzling of these instruments.

Indeed, nothing is more Baudelairean than woman as mirror or as reflector, the latter causing a multiplicity of lights to sparkle or shimmer; lights of which, if she is not the source, she is at least the present center of diffusion. In Baudelaire there is always a radiating *luce di femmina*, a strictly feminine luminosity which, like the illumination of cities at night, splits into an infinite number of fires:

> Soon, bathed by the disfused brilliance of a theater, receiving and casting light with their eyes, with their jewels, with their shoulders—appear, as dazzling as portraits in the theater box that serves to frame them, young women of high society.[130]

Yet this radiance of the feminine body—in itself or with its extraneous ornaments—is never so bright as when it is allied with its exact opposite: the dark quality of masculine thought. To dream of women is to illuminate one's own darkness. It is a beneficent light that at times, in casting its dazzling brilliance, brings appeasement and joy to the soul of one who is condemned to live in obscurity:

> Healer of my soul, you are
> Music, colour, living light!
> Warm explosion in the night
> Of my black Siberia!
>
> *Mon âme par toi guérie,*
> *Par toi, lumière et couleur!*
> *Explosion de chaleur*
> *Dans ma noire Sibérie!*[131]

In a text such as this, the dichotomy is extremely clear. It is the same kind of contrast between black and white so frequent in Petrarchan or baroque poetry. Nevertheless, Baudelairean po-

---

130. "Le Peintre de la vie moderne," 1186.
131. "Chanson d'après-midi," 58 (76, Alan Conder).

etry more often suggests an ambiguous complicity between light and night. Its ideal would be a substance both dark and luminous; a source of light and a principle of darkness. In the feminine realm this may be found in the form of a head of black hair—dark by definition, but doubly luminous since, when outspread, it reveals its luster and with its evocative power can call forth an image flooded with light. It is, on the one hand, "a sea of ebony"; and on the other, creator of a "dazzling" dream. In Baudelaire, verbal synthesis delights in uniting these contradictory qualities:

> Pavilion, of blue-shadowed tresses spun,
> You give me back the azure from afar
>
> *Cheveux bleus, pavillon de ténèbres tendues,*
> *Vous me rendez l'azur du ciel immense et rond.*[132]

Through the lens of memory, the sky is seen totally inverted, like an aerial landscape reflected in water. Instead of enveloping, from above and from the outside, the world upon which it extends its azure and discharges its light—the sky is here rigorously enclosed in a tent of dark hair, circumscribed by a canopy of darkness. Such is the magical effect of a woman's hair spreading out: to make the azure heavens the center of an interior universe whose walls are the night.

There are yet other focuses of internal light to be found in Baudelaire. Without a doubt, stimulants are among them. For those who use them, they light up a center of inward luminosity. Thus, in the eyes of the drunkard, wine visions are "illuminated by the interior sun."[133] In Baudelairean terms, sensual pleasure causes "a flame in our subterranean depths"[134] to arise. Sometimes this subterranean world is so completely severed from the outside world, so exclusively illuminated by its own fire, that something dangerously morbid is emitted, such as Sapphic love—the attempt at mutual illumination by two identicals, soon the cause of a conflagration. The tunnel of Sapphic love is a mine in which noxious gases ignite:

> the fever damps
> That filter in through every crannied vent
> Break out with marsh-fire into sudden lamps

132. "La Chevelure," 25 (33, Doreen Bell).
133. "Du vin et du haschisch," 325.   134. "La prière d'un païen," 167.

Par les fentes des murs des miasmes fiévreux
Filtrent en s'enflammant ainsi que des lanternes.[135]

In short, all deep movement in the life of the imagination tends for Baudelaire to reveal itself in the guise of a luminous current, illuminating the mind, and yet emanating from that which is most obscure within it. It is this undercurrent that Baudelaire so admired in *Madame Bovary,* calling it "a faculty of suffering, subterranean and in revolt, running through the whole book . . . a dark thread that illuminates—what the English call the *undercurrent*—and serves as a guide through that pandemoniac Capernaum of solitude."[136]

Let us then imagine a source of light that is at once a lamp, jewels, a subterranean place, and a river, where the fundamental blackness of thought combines with its opposite: the luminosity of dreams. This theme is most fully developed in "Rêve parisien," with the image of the subterranean river:

> And every colour, even black,
> Became prismatic, polished, bright;
> The liquid gave its glory back
> Mounted in iridescent light.

> *Et tout, même la couleur noire,*
> *Semblait fourbi, clair, irisé;*
> *Le liquide enchâssait sa gloire*
> *Dans le rayon cristallisé.*[137]

Luminosity is thus both bright and dark; subterranean and bathed in light; mobile and yet congealed in crystal. The conjunction of opposites is here pushed to the limit. Moreover, the autonomy of local light is nowhere else as clearly asserted. The poet is the author of an architecture of luminous fairylands, depending upon an exclusively internal principle of lighting:

> There was no moon, there was no sun,—
> For why should sun and moon conspire
> To light such prodigies?—each one
> Blazed with its own essential fire!

> *Nul astre d'ailleurs, nuls vestiges*
> *De soleil, même au bas du ciel,*

135. "Delphine et Hippolyte," 139 (155, Aldous Huxley).
136. "Madame Bovary," 657.
137. "Rêve parisien," 98 (130, Edna St. Vincent Millay).

Pour illuminer ces prodiges,
Qui brillaient d'un feu personne![138]

These words express the most explicit of ambitions. We may formulate this ambition by saying that the poet wants to make of light his property, his own possession, his personal affair. In order for this to be possible he must begin by imprisoning light, making it the prisoner of a closed world—the room, for example, in a place closed in by curtains or shutters:

I'll shut the doors and window-casements tight,
And build my faery palace in the night.

Je fermerai partout portières et volets
Pour bâtir dans la nuit mes féeriques palais.[141]

In order for the architect of the "faery palace" to succeed in erecting a truly enchanted edifice, he must first enclose the space to be illuminated. In this way, the light of day will not engage in competition with that of night. Night will be the authentic creator of light. Analogous to the night will be the beloved's gaze, which, like the black sun of Hugo, Nerval and the occultists, is a star both dark and luminous:

Her eyes are two caverns in which mystery gleams
mistily, and her gaze illuminates like lightening: it is
an explosion in the darkness. I should compare her to
a black sun . . . showering light and happiness.[140]

Succulent fruit of the night, flower of evil or of misfortune, "black and yet luminous"[141]—nocturnal light thus expresses a paradox fundamental to the Baudelairean world. Its complex character unites the two irreconcilable principles whose names are good and evil, beauty and ugliness, luminosity and obscurity. This "double and simultaneous postulation" may be found expressed simply by Baudelaire, in the form of an absolute contradiction. But at times he attempts to transcend contradiction, in order imaginatively to attain a vision in which the irreconcilable is reconciled and the contradictory unified. In these instances, Baudelaire is no longer presenting a real world where good lies in

138. Ibid.   139. "Paysage," 78 (105, F. P. Sturm).
140. "Le désir de peindre," 289.   141. "Les Ténèbres," 36.

evil, beauty in ugliness, and luminosity in obscurity. Rather, we find a world both supra- and infrareal, in which good is evil, beauty is ugliness, luminosity is obscurity. Need we be reminded that this world is that of the gnostics and occultists; a world where, through the inversion of values, goodness resides at the heart of evil, beauty at the heart of ugliness, and real light in darkness? Thus we no longer merely have light within night, light emanating from night; but we also have a light that is black, a light fundamentally dark. Such is the most radical conception of light as it is occasionally formulated by Baudelaire.

This conception can be found in a line from "Ténèbres": "It is She, black and yet luminous," and again in a sentence from the essay, "L'Œuvre et la vie de Delacroix": "The sensation is that a magical atmosphere has approached and enveloped you. Dark and yet exquisite, luminous but peaceful, this impression . . . settles in your memory forever."[142]

It can be found in "Rêve parisien," where everything, even the color black, seems prismatic, polished, and bright.

It can be found in "L'Irrémédiable," a poem about self-confrontation, in which the eyes, phosphoric eyes, of viscous monsters, "make even blacker still the night," symbolizing thought's dialogue with itself:

> The dialogue is dark and clear
> When a heart becomes its mirror!
> Black well of Truth, but none is clearer,
> Where that livid star appears.
>
> *Tête-à-tête sombre et limpide*
> *Qu'un coeur devenu son miroir!*
> *Puits de Vérité, clair et noir,*
> *Où tremble une étoile livide.*[143]

As in the dark staircase of "Igitur," where, for Mallarmé, polished panels form mirrors endlessly casting between themselves the reflection of the figure descending the stairs, so Baudelairean thought, too, sinks into this confrontation, into this identification of light and shadow, to attain a region where night is no longer only the author of light, but light the author of night.

This ultimate region is at the very core of hell. For Baudelaire,

---

142. "L'Œuvre et la vie de Delacroix," 1125.
143. "L'Irrémédiable," 76 (99, Henry Curwen).

nocturnal light can finally be conceptualized only as light from below. It is the Luciferian light, darkly illuminating an understanding which knows itself to be the understanding of evil. It is thus an ironic understanding.

Lucid and black, obscurely lucid, such is "consciousness in evil":

> That ironic primaeval
> Beacon, torch of Satan's grace . . .

> *Un phare ironique, infernal,*
> *Flambeau des grâces sataniques . . .*[144]

In contrast to divine light which, in Augustinian and Franciscan thought, renders the world intelligible by illuminating it with a light celestial in the eyes of saintly understanding, there is, then, a demonic light which makes the world ironically comprehensible to a truly demonic consciousness.

What we may term the temptation of Baudelaire consists then in this: the temptation to use black light as a source of knowledge, of power, and of pleasure. It is from this demonic perspective that he chooses to view the world:

"Against a backdrop of demonic light or of the aurora borealis" (which Baudelaire elsewhere terms "the reflection of hell's fireworks"), "red, orange, sulphurous, pink, at times violet—against these magical backdrops, variously imitating Bengal lights, there emerges the variegated image of illicit beauty."[145]

> . . . your red rays reflect the hell,
> In which my heart is pleased to dwell.

> . . . *Vos lueurs sont le reflet*
> *De l'Enfer où mon coeur se plaît.*[146]

And yet is there not in Baudelaire the dream of another kind of light? Emerging from far beyond, from beneath all subterranean and underwater visions of black light—the lost jewels of ancient Palmyra, unknown metals, pearls of the sea—there is for Baudelaire the conception of a world of pure light, a light no longer coupled with darkness, its radiance no longer a satanic irony. Pure light, rendering all things divinely intelligible, is, as

---

144. Ibid.   145. "Le Peintre de la vie moderne," 1187.
146. "Horreur sympathique," 73 (96, Roy Campbell).

we have just noted, the very conception of Augustinian illuminism. Let us remember the image of the diadem, "dazzling and bright," ending the poem that opens *Les Fleurs du mal:*

> For Thou knowest it will be made of purest light
> Drawn from the holy hearth of every primal ray,
> To which all human eyes, if they were one bright
> Eye, are only a tarnished mirror's fading day!
>
> *Car il ne sera fait que de pure lumière,*
> *Puisée au foyer saint des rayons primitifs,*
> *Et dont les yeux mortels, dans leur splendeur entière,*
> *Ne sont que des miroirs obscurcis et plaintifs.*[147]

No ambiguity is possible here. No confusion can arise between the pure light drawn from the holy hearth and the black light originating from the obscure depths of being. There can be no imaginable compromise between the light from above and that from below. The only remaining possibility for dark light to approach pure light is by becoming the latter's reflection, its obscured mirror. Baudelaire's philosophy of light obeys the same laws as his aesthetics. It is a philosophy that ultimately expresses the condition of man, dreaming the perfect into the imperfect.

3

IN THE PROSE POEM "Les Yeux des pauvres," Baudelaire formulates a dream, the realization of which would be no less essential to his happiness than the union of his thought with nature, or of light with night.

That dream is of the union of his thought with the thought of others.

Baudelaire writes of himself and his mistress in a prose poem:

> We had indeed promised each other that all our thoughts would be open to one another, and that henceforth our two souls would make but one.[148]

147. "Bénédiction," 9 (9–10, David Paul).
148. "Les Yeux des pauvres," 268.

The two lovers aspire to attain a total intercommunication. Each will reflect the other's feelings. The mirror of the eyes will serve as guarantor. By gazing deep into his beloved's eyes, the lover will read his own thoughts. Reciprocation will be genuine on both sides. Thus the lover and his mistress will exchange a single process of thought. By virtue of this conjunction of two modes of feeling and of understanding (an understanding of *oneself*), a harmony will arise between the two souls. They will be conscious of it. This harmony is on the same order as that attained by the poet in his paradisiac moments, when he gains awareness of the analogy existing between himself and supernaturalized nature.

In this Baudelaire poem, however, the identification ends in failure. The thoughts of the beloved prove to be radically different from those of the poet. Far from mutually reflecting each other the two minds assert their difference. The poet concludes that "thought is incommunicable, even between lovers."

In any case, Baudelaire is forced to acknowledge the fundamental solitude of man. To be born is to be severed from some kind of ineffable union; to be thrown out into a world in which comprehension between individuals, even between mother and son, is impossible. In 1839, Baudelaire writes to his mother, "And when I feel within myself something that uplifts me—who knows what: a violent desire to kiss everything, or simply a beautiful sunset seen from a window—*with whom can I share it?*" With whom, is the implication, if not with you? Indeed, to be able to confide it immediately to his mother would reassure and appease him. But the question has an uneasy inflection. Even if the mother were present, it would be difficult, perhaps even impossible, to communicate what is felt. It may be that, even in her son's presence, the mother is always absent; and the same may hold true for friends, mistresses, and all the individuals who instill in us the desire to forget, when they are with us, that we are alone.

Human solitude is universal. Like everything else, it is a consequence of original sin. Solitude is part of that general destiny that prevents us from living harmoniously with a corrupt nature and those who inhabit it.

Any breach of this solitude is illusion.

"In love as in almost all of human affairs, cordial relations are the result of a misunderstanding. That misunderstanding is pleasure. The man cries out, 'Oh, my angel,' and the woman coos, "Mother, Mother," and both of these imbeciles are convinced they are thinking in unison.—And the unfathomable abyss remains intact."[149]

The chasm that yawns between man and his fellow creatures is thus no less gaping than the one separating him from a world with which he is no longer in harmony. Human beings are each other's chasms. An absolute distance stretches out between them; a rigid boundary closes them in on themselves. Just as there is a ceiling that imposes itself between thought and free space, so too there is a screen that makes individuals impenetrable to each other.

What, then, is to be done? Accept the condition of a corrupt nature? Resign oneself to eternal solitude? Or, worse still, accept that one's relations with others will never be anything but ambiguous or hostile? Baudelaire is often tempted to accept this latter solution. He often practices irony or hatred in his contact with others. Here is irony:

> The man of acumen—the one who will never be reconciled to anyone—must apply himself to animating the conversation of idiots and the reading of bad books. He will glean bitter satisfaction from this undertaking.[150]

And here, hatred:

> I must tell all: I have an arrogance that sustains me, and a savage hatred for all men. I always hope to dominate, to take my revenge.[151]

At times sarcastic, at other times violently aggressive, Baudelaire's misanthropy is universal. It lashes out against all individuals, finding cause for resentment or contempt everywhere. Man constantly and ubiquitously offers "the tedious spectacle of eternal sin." Hence we have the proof, as far as humans are concerned, of a wretched equality. All are jointly responsible for the same offense. Extending the sentiment of this solidarity or similarity in evil even to God himself (as preached by

---

149. "Mon coeur mis à nu," 1289.   150. Ibid., 1298.
151. "A sa mère," 12 October 1860.

Joseph de Maistre), Baudelaire sees strangers everywhere; strangers who are nonetheless intimately associated through a hideous equivalence.

The concept of this equivalence prompts the poet to say to his mistress, "So long as your dreams have not mirrored hell . . . so long as you have not felt the embrace of irresistable repulsion, you [will not have the right to] say to me: I am your equal."[152]

In a poem entitled "Assommons les pauvres," Baudelaire tells the story of having once beaten a poor man in order to force him into beating the poet black and blue in return. Afterward, Baudelaire says to the poor man, "Sir, you are my equal."[153]

So there is equality in shame, in vice, in violence, and perhaps in crime as well: "We are all hanged or fit to be hanged."[154] Yet herein lies an unexpected means for establishing contact with one another. All men are our doubles, our fellow creatures. Despite the law of incommunicability, which seems to affect us similarly, the resemblance between our natures (the natures of fallen beings) and the analogous quality of our behavior offer a final chance for comparing our lives and, thus, for understanding one another.

The famous challenge with which *Les Fleurs du mal* begins is well known: "Hypocrite reader, you—my double! my brother!"

This challenge is to be taken very seriously and literally. Precisely because the reader is the poet's double and brother, he will be able to understand the voice addressing him. The poet appeals to the brotherhood in evil of all those who, like him, feel themselves to be at once culprit and victim. They are all similar. Deep within himself, every individual knows that he can rely upon the comprehension of others. In another poem, turning once again to the reader, Baudelaire gives him this command, which merely develops the preceding words:

> But if, not yielding to their charm,
> Your eye can plumb the gulfs of harm—
> Then learn to love me, read my verses.
> Pity me! . . . else, receive my curses!

---

152. "Madrigal triste," 170.   153. "Assommons les pauvres," 306.
154. "Projets de préface," 184.

Mais si, sans se laisser charmer,
Ton œil sait plonger dans les gouffres;
Lis-moi pour apprendre à m'aimer;
Plains-moi! . . . Sinon je te maudis.[155]

The hypocritical reader is thus called upon to pity and even to love the poet, in whom he discovers the same propensity for the abyss as his own. He and the author he reads are both speleologists, both explorers of chasms. They recognize in each other the same experiences, and the same taste. Will this sentiment perhaps allow them more readily to feel a mutual, understanding sympathy? There is then a possibility of overcoming the obstacle of solitude, and of achieving comprehension and empathy. Evil accompanied by suffering can at times inspire pity—a pity even akin to a kind of love. Baudelaire dreams of finding female consolation: guardian angels, muses, or madonnas. He imagines them giving him courage, guiding his steps. His lips repeat a name: Electra. She is the criminal's sister, who soothes his blood-stained dreams and wipes his sweat-bathed brow. She is closely tied to her brother because of the compassion aroused in her by the knowledge of the dark depths into which the murderer's thoughts stray. A type of knowledge settles itself between men, those beings of such unhappy solitude—a knowledge based on the crimes they have committed and the evils they have endured. The first way of overcoming universal incommunicability is through the complicity of pity.

Is this not the same situation we find in the moving passage from the *Journaux intimes?* Here we see Baudelaire and his mistress, filled with compassion at the thought of their life together—full of errors and quarrels as it may have been—combining their tears: "She shuddered; she too felt compassion and was moved."[156] Here, in the mutual understanding of the "profound years," something quite different from hostility or irony emerges; something which, emerging from the bowels of discord, restores harmony to disjointed souls.

Perhaps it is the rougher sketch of this gesture that we distinguish in a scene from the *Poèmes en prose.* Here we see Baudelaire looking through a garret window at "a mature wom-

155. "Epigraphe pour un livre condamné," 163 (189, Roy Campbell).
156. "Fusées," 1261.

an, already wrinkled, poor, always bent over something, and who never goes out." To this portrait Baudelaire adds the following notation: "With her face, her clothes, her gestures, with almost nothing at all, *I have rewritten this woman's story*, or rather, her legend."

There is no doubt a great difference between two lovers united by the memory of their life together and the partial identification of the poet with an unknown woman whose past he imagines. Yet in both cases the identification depends upon the participation of one of those minds in the experience of the other, perceived or conceived in all of its profundity. It appears that, for Baudelaire the real way of getting out of oneself and of uniting with that eternal stranger (which is what the other always is for us), is to merge with him into his story.

Baudelaire's continually recurring need to mingle in the daily life of others, "to wed the crowd,"[157] is well known. Nothing contrasts more sharply with the sense of incommunicability he experiences at other times. "For then the poet," he says, "enjoys that incomparable privilege of being himself and others at will. Like those wandering souls in search of a body, he can, when he wishes, enter into the mind of anyone."[158]

It is true that here one might think the sentiment entirely different in kind from that in the preceding examples. Is not an identification with a sentiment purely gregarious in nature? Is not what is desired here a "fraternity of prostitution," to invoke the phrase Baudelaire employs somewhere?

The desire to merge with the crowd, however, should not be confused with the need to identify with the plurality of individuals who constitute that crowd. "The pleasure of being in crowds," writes Baudelaire, is the expression of the mysterious delight in "the multiplication of number." Poets, dandies, painters, or sketchers, prepared as they are to catch an expression, to sketch a gesture, consort with crowds because they find in crowds a moving manifestation of human experiences. Far from sweeping over the undifferentiated masses with a glance or a thought, they *scrutinize* with surprising rapidity the individuals who by turns attract their interest. "The lover of universal life

157. "Le Peintre de la vie moderne," 1160.   158. "Les Foules," 244.

enters into the crowd as he would into a vast electrical condenser. He may be . . . compared to a mirror as vast as that crowd; or to a kaleidoscope gifted with consciousness which, in every one of its movements, represents the manifold life and moving grace of all elements of existence."[159]

In a word, the experience of the crowd in all its swaying multiplicity is that of the human number. It is humanity in its aggregate offering itself to observation. But this aggregate is not perceived as a totality; it is simply a composite multiplicity, each element of which, taken in isolation, attracts scrutiny and reveals an individual life. There is, then, no fundamental difference between the way Baudelaire's mind "weds the crowd" and the way he espouses each particular life. No; the genuinely significant phenomenon is this: Baudelaire's ability—like that of certain writers or artists (Brueghel, Balzac, Delacroix, Constantin Guys)—to be passionately interested in the individuals who are the object of his attention. Then incommunicability no longer reigns. With a single impulse, first seizing upon the physical traits in order to infer the moral ones, Baudelaire's gaze and thought can penetrate individuals to their very core.

The most obvious example of this phenomenon is the poem "Les Petites Vieilles." In "sinuous folds of cities old and grim," the poet's gaze falls upon old women, contorted monsters. He sees in them "a taste both charming and bizarre." Curiosity motivates him to observe their gestures, their behavior, the wrinkles on their faces. Then the whole previous existence of these individuals, in all its intimacy, opens to his gaze:

> Sombre or bright, I see your vanished prime;
> My soul, resplendent with your virtue, blazes,
> And revels in your vices and your crimes.
>
> *Sombres ou lumineux, je vis vos jours perdus;*
> *Mon cœur multiplié jouit de tous vos vices!*
> *Mon âme resplendit de toutes vos vertus!*[160]

Vices and virtues which, in their youth, these wretched old women had once practiced, and which now become once again—not in them but in their observer's imagination—sources of joy

159. "Le Peintre de la vie moderne," 1160.
160. "Les Petites Vieilles," 87 (116–17, Roy Campbell).

and objects of splendor. Thus an identification has taken place between the old women and the observer. The latter has begun to relive their feelings in his mind. And this identification is so complete that it involves the resurrection in him of the vices and virtues that were once theirs.

Contrary to what most are inclined to believe, Baudelaire on more than one occasion shows himself to be the opposite of an egotist, if one understands this term to mean someone incapable of going outside of himself, someone solely absorbed by his ego. In contrast to those who usually have only a condescending, hasty, and superficial interest in others, Baudelaire finds within himself enough of a generous impulse to immerse himself into the life of another, and to live it in all its historical plenitude.

It would be wrong to limit Baudelaire's talent for identification to that of an actor. There is no doubt, as he himself says of his alter ego, Samuel Cramer, that Baudelaire is gifted with an "acting ability." The actor, consumed by his role, stands in front of the mirror in order to comtemplate, with his mimicry, gestures, and facial expression, the "new personality that must become his own." But the identification is not merely an external mimeticism; for the actor must double as historian. A portrait painter does not only depict the face. He paints an existence stretched out over time. Intuition into others goes far beyond appearances. It entails following and, even more importantly, *becoming* an individual over a span of years, including the genesis and development of his destiny.

But how can this be? What process allows for moving from a state of absolute solitude to that extraordinary penetration into the private life of others?

The answer to this question is of great importance, for it hinges upon the significance that can be granted to all of Baudelaire's critical and aesthetic thought and, in particular, to his notion of harmony and analogy.

One kind of harmony, in Baudelaire's sense of the term, is that existing between the different parts of a given object. Harmony thus viewed appears as the interrelation of the elements of which the object is made up. Let us consider a Delacroix painting. It is perceived in its harmony when the different means of expression used by the painter seem to operate for the purpose of revealing their analogy to the spectator. Between the colors and the designs and, even more, between the particular hues of coloration and the sinuous and varied strokes of the designs, an indefinable identity emerges. To view a Delacroix painting is to replace the scrutiny of parts, from an analytical and dissecting perspective, with a synthetic vision. Such a vision is possible only if the spectator's gaze moves from the perception of parts to that of the whole. The eye recognizes in each of these parts a resemblance to all the rest. Without this act of recognition, there would be no general comprehension of the painting.

In the same way, for Baudelaire a woman's beauty is perceptible within the impression of a generalized harmony, present in every aspect of her being. Every particular detail functions in unison with all the others to make her unique type of beauty *recognizable:*

> The harmony is far too great,
> That governs all her body fair,
> For impotence to analyse
> And say which note is sweetest there.
>
> O mystic metamorphosis!
> My senses into one sense flow—
> Her voice makes perfume when she speaks,
> Her breath is music faint and low!
>
> *Et l'harmonie est trop exquise*
> *Qui gouverne tout son beau corps,*
> *Pour que l'impuissante analyse*
> *En note les nombreux accords.*
>
> *O métamorphose mystique*
> *De tous mes sens fondus en un!*
> *Son haleine fait la musique*
> *Comme sa voix fait le parfum!*[161]

Woman is thus a perpetual metaphor. Each of her allurements echoes all the others. Synaesthesia is the means by which her charms may be transformed into yet new ones. She appears as the synthesis of discrete parts, which identify with each other. In order for this transposition to occur, the mind of a contemplator must be at work. Woman is a painting that must undergo, in the spectator's mind, what Baudelaire calls a "mystic meta-

---

161. "Tout entière," 40 (52–53, F. P. Sturm).

morphosis" to gain its full value. Observation, then, by an act of
both imagination and memory (appealing to all the stored memories one possesses), is the discovery within oneself of a series of
equivalents for the observed object. This holds true even for the
most disconcerting of objects, and even for the ugliest. If I admire
a painting by Goya, it is because the contortions and grimaces of
the diabolical figures I see before me first reveal to me "the analogy and harmony that exist objectively in all aspects of these
beings." But, second, it is because all of these figures, despite
their savage faces, "are imbued with humanity." In spite of their
hideousness—or perhaps because of it—they reveal their resemblance to their observer. He is linked to them through personal interest.

The universal analogy is manifest in thousands of ways. The
transposition of objective reality into a mental image is effected in
thousands of ways. The woman who knows this is she who, by
her clothing and makeup—that is, by a "sublime deformation of
nature"—becomes, in the eyes of her admirers, "magical and
supernatural." The same holds true for nature, certainly debased
and corrupt, but always ready to "reclothe herself in a supernatural intrigue" when viewed in her totality. Thus Delacroix's
paintings, like Poe's poetry, are "translations" that introject supernaturalism into objective reality.

This supernaturalizing of nature is never so clear in Baudelaire
as in his descriptions of cities. The very act of walking in the city
makes mystery and enchantment emerge at every step:

> Ant-seething city, city full of dreams,
> Where ghosts by daylight tug the passer's sleeve.
> Mystery, like sap, through all its conduit-streams,
> Quickens the dread Colossus that they weave.

> *Fourmillante cité, cité pleine de rêves,*
> *Où le spectre en plein jour raccroche le passant!*
> *Les mystères partout coulent comme des sèves*
> *Dans les canaux étroits du colosse puissant.*[162]

In Baudelaire there is a realism of the fantastic that has its
origins, as he admits himself, in the landscapes of painters. He
loves the "great lakes that represent immobility in despair; the

162. "Les Sept Vieillards," 83 (111, Roy Campbell).

huge mountains, the planet's stairway to the sky . . . ; fortified castles; crenelated monasteries . . . ; enormous bridges; Ninevite constructions, inhabited by vertigo." It is this supernaturalism which prevents Baudelaire from taking much pleasure in the landscape artists of the French school (with the exception of Corot and Théodore Rousseau). He sees them as "overly herbivorous animals." He does not like "irregular plant life." On the other hand, he does like stone and landscapes of stone. Hence his preference for painters and engravers who invent fantastic cities.

We have already said that it is impossible to find even the slightest mention of Piranesi in the works of Baudelaire. And yet, in his description of opium-produced dreams, what he evokes is indeed a Piranesian vision:

> Astonishing and monstrous edifices arose in his brain . . . Dreams of terraces, towers, ramparts, rising to unknown heights and sinking into vast depths.[163]

There can be no doubt but that this is a Piranesian dream, though not inspired directly by the etcher's plates. It is doubtless informed by the reading of De Quincey, who had already marvelously transposed the Piranesian fantastic into prose—prose that Baudelaire translated.

Here is another passage in which the urban fantastic seems for Baudelaire to spring from another source. This passage is to be found both in the *Salon de 1859* and in the essay on Gautier. There is, says Baudelaire, a painter, a "dreamy architect," whose name half escapes him (it is in fact the English painter E. H. Kendall), who "builds cities on paper; cities with bridges of elephant pillars, letting gigantic three-masted ships pass between the elephant legs at full sail."

The following vision is again Piranesian. It is the notation of a dream which Baudelaire perhaps considered making into a prose poem:

> Symptoms of ruin. Enormous edifices. Several lying on top of each other: apartments, rooms, temples, galleries, staircases, caeca, belvederes, lanterns, fountains, statues.—Fissures, crevices, humidity coming from a reservoir situated near the sky . . . At the very

163. "Les Paradis artificiels," 428.

top, a column splits and both its extremities move.
Nothing has yet collapsed. I can no longer find the
way out.[164]

But if the urban fantastic of Baudelaire seems indirectly or
directly Piranesian in origin, it is in another great artist—this time
a contemporary—that he finds the most precise equivalent of his
supernaturalism. The urban landscapes of Méryon lack the huge
and violently dramatic quality of Piranesi's etchings. But they
have the same power of suggestion, and the same capacity to
transform the real into an authentically poetic image.

Baudelaire writes about Méryon:

> I have rarely seen the natural solemnity of a huge
> city represented more poetically. The majesty of piled-
> up stone; bell towers pointing to the sky; the obelisks
> of industry vomiting their coalitions of smoke into the
> firmament; the prodigious scaffoldings of monuments
> under repair, overlaying the solid body of the architec-
> ture with their own architecture of openwork, of such
> paradoxical beauty; the tumultuous sky teeming with
> rage and resentment; the depth of perspective height-
> ened by the thought of all the dramas contained with-
> in it—none of the complex elements making up the
> painful and glorious decor of civilization were
> omitted.[165]

It is clear why Baudelaire manifests such a predilection for Méryon's etchings: they unite the "depth of perspective" with the
"complexity" of elements. Depth and complexity, as we have
noted more than once, are the essential traits of Baudelairean
poetry. They are also those of the Méryonesque drawing: depth
rendered complex by the thought of all the dramas contained
within these vast decors.

Indeed, a city does not consist solely of various kinds of architecture. It is also made up of the individuals who inhabit it.
Baudelaire, who loves the multiple individuals he encounters in
the city crowd, admires the painters and sketchers who capture
those fleeting apparitions. These artists are Hogarth, Charlet,
Gavarni, Constantin Guys. But above all there is Daumier, the
Goya of city life:

164. "Spleen de Paris," 317.   165. "Salon de 1859," 1083.

Peruse his work, and you will see a procession before your eyes; a procession of all the living mon-
strosities that a great city, with all its fantastic and
gripping reality, can contain. Everything it harbors in
the way of terrifying, grotesque, sinister, and farcical
treasures—Daumier knows.[166]

Thus, through a process that is constantly repeated, Baudelaire, facing a canvas he admires, is not content to appreciate
form and color from the outside. His own world corresponds to
the fantastic world of the canvas. An entire world of "terrifying
treasures" also inhabits Baudelaire's mind. The grimacing population that peoples the artist's canvases, and the images that
obsess the poet, reveal their essential sameness.

The poet is therefore not only a poet. He is the one from whom
there emerges a network of images analogous to the vision of
others,—a type of secondary image; an action by which, as critic,
Baudelaire turns himself into the respondent to works which
speak to him.

There is no doubt that Baudelaire is a great critic; the greatest of
his time. But it remains perhaps unclear why he is so great. It is
because his critical process differs in no way from his poetic one.
Baudelaire is the only writer who continually uses his imagination in his criticism as well as in his poetry. These two literary
genres overlap for him. His poetry is a critical poetry, just as his
criticism is a poetic one.

This may be seen clearly in the process of identification by
which Baudelaire recreates or retrieves within himself the analogous equivalent of the book he reads or the theatrical perfor-
mance he attends. Such is in fact the final aspect of Baudelaire
that remains for us to consider: the phenomenon of critical identification, so close to that of poetic identification. Let us recall the
poem "Les Petites Vieilles," the apparition of those specters, the
attention given them by the poet, the intuition with which he
genuinely immerses himself in their existence, remembering
their past as if it were his own. Is this not the same procedure as
the one in which Baudelaire *submits himself to* Delacroix's painting, which, like Baudelaire's own poetry, is essentially sug-
gestive? Delacroix's works "return to memory the greatest of

166. "Quelques caricaturistes," 1004.

poetic feelings and ideas which one had thought lost forever in the night of the past."

The poet's creative mnemotechny thus corresponds to the re-creating capacity of the critic's memory and imagination. In reference, not to Delacroix, but to another artist, Constantin Guys, Baudelaire makes the following observation: "[the painter], in faithfully translating his own impressions, imprints the culminating or luminous aspects of any object with an instinctive energy . . . and the spectator's imagination, submitting in turn to this despotic mnemotechny, sees with great clarity the impression that objects have made in the mind of M. Guys. The spectator is here the translator of a translation."[167]

Translator of a translation: the expression is marvelously accurate. But it must be grasped in its intended meaning. The critic is no more content than the painter to limit himself to a slavish copy. He does not reproduce—how could he?—the forms and colors of the painting that interests him. But these forms and colors will become a language for him, depicting a host of emotions, ideas, and an entire life of imagination, the equivalent of which he will endeavor to find in himself. Corresponding to the profound life of the painter, the life inscribed on his canvas, there is another life—also profound and harking back to an individual past: the profound, personal life of the critic. One will answer for the other; both will become echoes.

What holds true in the realm of art criticism does so equally in that of music or literary criticism. Of the overture to *Tannhäuser* and its effect on the audience, Baudelaire notes: "Every man of flesh and blood *who remembers* begins to tremble. Every well-shaped brain carries within itself two infinites: heaven and hell. And in every representation of these two infinites, he suddenly recognizes his other half!"[168]

The equivalent of the duality in Wagner's work is thus the spiritual duality of its listener. Each serves as the symbol of the other. And the fullness of meaning contained in the strictly musical work will find its fulfillment only if, at the moment of its realization as sound, a corresponding movement occurs silently in the soul of the listener.

167. "Le Peintre de la vie moderne," 1166.
168. "Richard Wagner et Tannhäuser," 1224.

Music awakens in him the poem of his life. Poetry does so as well. To read a poem is to put oneself in a situation which, in readerly thought, allows for the reliving of feelings analogous to those which inspired the poem. In any case, such is Baudelaire's profound conviction. He affirms it with great emphasis. In reference to the poetry of Marceline Desbordes-Valmore, he notes: "The torch that she waves before our eyes to illuminate the mysterious copse of feeling, or which she puts close to our most intimate memory as lovers or sons, to revive it—that torch has been lit in the profoundest depths of her own heart."[169]

Because of the luminous magic of words, two affective depths are illuminated in turn: first, the emotion ignited in the heart of the poetess; second—analogous to it but situated in the mental depths of another mind—the emotion her reader (here, Baudelaire) associates with the most intimate of his own memories.

The mnemotechny of art is then double: for the painter, musician, poet, it revives the experience they once personally lived, and which they need to form the substance of their work. And it returns to the reader, listener, spectator (that is, the critic), a corresponding personal experience.

Nevertheless, this dual resuscitation of the past must not be seen as a matter strictly of memory (even of affective memory). It has rather to do with an intervention on the part of the power of the imagination, linked to former emotions.

"Real memory," says Hoffmann in a text quoted by Baudelaire, "consists only, I believe, in a vivid imagination that is easily moved and, consequently, able to evoke scenes from the past with the help of each sensation, by granting to each of them—as if by magic—a life and personality of their own."[170]

The best critic is therefore the one who succeeds in creating in himself, through an act of imagination aided by memory, a type of response analogous to the work he has read or contemplated— or, at the very least, analogous to the work's affective and intellectual contents. And such is precisely the fundamental direction of Baudelaire's thought. Even when he does not look critically upon a work, even when he seeks in it, as often happens to him, a

169. "Marceline Desbordes-Valmore," 719.
170. "Salon de 1846," 927, note.

source of personal inspiration, he cannot stop his imagination from visualizing what it is creating, like the echo or reflection of the work he has admired. Between the latter and his own work, there arise such striking similarities that Baudelaire himself, re-reading his own writing after the fact, is unable to make the distinction between what has come to him from the outside and what is the result of his own genius. Referring to his essay on "Les Paradis artificiels" and, in particular, to the second half of that work, which is heavily influenced by De Quincey's text, Baudelaire admits that he has "added personal remarks here and there" to his translation. But, he adds, "I would be hard pressed to say how big a dose of my own personality has been injected into the original author."[171]

This uncertainty is to be found in Baudelaire with respect to all the writers who influenced him. When he discovers Edgar Allen Poe, he first feels "a singular commotion."[172] He discovers an "intimate resemblance" between Poe's work and his own.[173] This resemblance matters to him above all else and becomes, from the moment he is aware of it, the fundamental reason he continually returns to Poe, making him his master and inspiration. And yet, before he had even read Poe, Baudelaire was already writing poems so similar to Poe's that one could mistake them for translations. Why then the great attachment to Poe and his work, given that Baudelaire already possessed all that they communicated to him? The answer to this question is a simple one. If Baudelaire constantly returns to Poe, it is not because Poe offers him something new. On the contrary, it is because he finds in Poe the equivalent of what he finds in himself. Poe is his correspondent; the one with whom he maintains a close rapport of symmetry and similitude.

For Baudelaire, the creative act almost always depends upon a mirror effect; upon a likeness that he recognizes between himself and another artist. Baudelaire thinks, one day, about writing prose poems. He discovers a certain similarity between what he is thinking of doing and Aloysius Bertrand's famous *Gaspard de la nuit*. In rereading this work, he says he is moved "to attempt something analogous."[174] It matters little that, when *Spleen de*

---

171. "Les Paradis artificiels," 463.   172. "A Armand Fraisse," 1858.
173. "A sa mère," 8 March 1854.   174. "Préface au Spleen de Paris," 229.

Paris is drafted, it proves itself to be a work of a distinctly different kind. What is significant is that Baudelaire takes an analogy as his point of departure. Another example: in rereading the poetry of Marceline Desbordes-Valmore, Baudelaire rediscovers her with the eyes of the adolescent he had been upon reading her for the first time. It is in the dreams of his distant past that he can recover the immediacy of Marceline's dreams. What is at issue here is not a fortuitous similarity, accepted docilely—and thus superficially. Were that the case, the similarity would have remained sterile. Baudelaire's imagination must *act* upon this resemblance and transform it into a metaphorical equivalent: "I dream," he writes, "of what Mme. Valmore's poetry made me feel when I read it with those adolescent eyes which are, for sensitive men, both so passionate and so clairvoyant." Such is the still passive and receptive stance of the simple reader. But now comes the transformation of the reader's stance into an act that is overtly critical: "This poetry," Baudelaire continues, "appears before me like a garden." It is an English garden, romantic and romanesque, with sinuous and shaded alleys whose meanderings "open up onto huge vistas of the past or future.[175]

Huge vistas! Need we emphasize the analogy between the profundity Baudelaire *reads into* the poetry of Marceline Desbordes-Valmore and the profundity that is the fundamental trait of his own poetry? In reading Valmore and imagining her own frail genius, Baudelaire once again finds a means of representing his own genius metaphorically—or, rather, of finding between her and himself the common denominator that allows him, through a more advanced knowledge of others, a better grasp of his own thought. Baudelaire proceeds in the same manner with the painters who, in his *Salons*, are subject to an unforgettable critical interpretation.

Whether seen together or taken separately, they offer, from a certain point of view, a series of metaphorical equivalents for the Baudelairean world.

That world appears then, not as isolated or limited to a single mind, but as being preceded, enriched, and supported by an entire procession of precursory minds, which have already offered similar versions of Baudelaire's perspective. Baudelaire, so

175. "Marceline Desbordes-Valmore," 721.

tragically isolated in his personal life, wants to be surrounded in his life as a writer by poets and artists—surrounded by doubles, those who possess an imagination, with a way of feeling and thinking approximating his own. These he calls "beacons." At night, along the banks of a river, a number of specks of light can be discerned, projecting beams of light to great distances. They are isolated and yet connected because they resemble each other. For Baudelaire, great artists, like great poets, are similar to those luminous points which, each arranged at an unequal but fixed distance from the other, form a chain that the mind moves along, ascertaining resemblances. "Beacons" are for him part of the vast universal analogy he discovers between his own mind and the world; between his own mind and those who precede him in exploiting the riches of analogical truth. And because that truth reveals itself indirectly, through a continual reflection upon itself and in a series of mirrors and echoes, it is not surprising that Baudelaire's analogical world presents itself as an unceasingly reiterated and unceasingly retransmitted statement; one repeated by a thousand labyrinths, and echoed by a thousand megaphones.

Rimbaud

For his part, the poet tries to reconstruct the act of creation.
—Marcel Raymond[1]

1. Marcel Raymond, *De Baudelaire au surréalisme* (Paris: Corti, 1952), 42.

4

In *Une saison en enfer,* Rimbaud, summing up his life, makes the following observation:

> I see my spirit is sleeping.
> If it were always wide awake from this moment on, we would soon reach truth, who perhaps surrounds us with her weeping angels! . . . If it had been awake until this moment, I would not have given in to my deleterious instincts at an immemorial time! . . . —If it had always been awake, I would be sailing in full wisdom![2]

There was then a moment, the poet remembers, when his mind was fully awake; when it was in a position to approach wisdom; when it could hope not only to attain truth but to retain it as well. That initial moment, from which time it seemed to him that his mind could remain indefatigably active, was the moment of waking. Such an awakening would not have limited itself to that brief instant which follows sleep, but would have had the power to prolong itself indefinitely and without flagging—as if the poet, merely by opening his eyes, were to acquire simultaneously the privilege of being eternally aware of what his understanding reveals to him and of what falls beneath his gaze.

An uninterrupted waking, never ceasing, promising from the outset to be eternal—here is the fundamental hope cherished by Rimbaud. To awaken, to be born at a given moment into the sensation of existence,—would this not also entail the assurance that this feeling is destined to remain unchanged, uninterrupted, unabated, during the whole of existence? A feeling intact, ever active, bearing the totality of its riches, but also the amplitude and all the intense joy its enjoyment can procure? To pursue forever the act of waking, to remain continually the possessor of all that this brief moment can grant us—this appears to have been Rimbaud's first ambition. But he soon concludes that this ambition is fundamentally illusory. There can be no uninterrupted awakening, nor an indefinitely prolonged state of the gaining of consciousness. Waking is not a permanent state, an unchanging

2. *Une saison en enfer,* 237 (205).

mode of existence; nor is it an unalterable way of life. It is the instantaneous acquisition of consciousness, at times an over-whelming one, but strictly ephemeral. Therein may lie the reason that the angels, to which Rimbaud refers in the text cited above, in perceiving the fleeting nature of the revelations that waking brings to humans, shed tears of compassion upon them and their fate. Man is condemned to profit by his morning illuminations in brief moments only; moments severed by interruptions. More-over, every man longs for the awakenings he has enjoyed, and at times despairs of experiencing such moments again.

These regrets, these deceptions—but also the retrieval of unex-pected joys in moments when one awakens anew, having almost lost the sensation of previous awakenings (and, in particular, those experienced in the prime of youth)—form the subject of one of Rimbaud's earliest poems, perhaps the first in which he is conscious of what separates the wakings of the past from those of the present. I am referring to "Les Etrennes des orphelins," dated 1869.

In that work Rimbaud portrays two orphans still sleeping at the dawn of a day that promises to be sad and lacking in all the joy that had once warmed their morning waking. Now they are with-out parents, without a home, deprived of heat and, almost, of life itself. It is against this backdrop of night, of absence, of separa-tion, of heavy and melancholy sleep, that the poet describes an awakening in the childrens' souls. It is not a true awakening, one that would magically restore to them everything of which they have been robbed; but a dreamed waking, an imaginary waking, of which they would discover themselves to be the happy beneficiaries:

> But the angel of cradles comes to wipe their eyes,
> And into their heavy sleep puts a happy dream,
> So happy a dream that their half-closed lips,
> Smiling, seem to murmur something . . .
> —They dream that, leaning on their small round arms,
> In the sweet gesture of waking up, they raise their heads,
> And peer around them . . .

> *Mais l'ange des berceaux vient essuyer leurs yeux,*
> *Et dans ce lourd sommeil met un rêve joyeux,*
> *Un rêve si joyeux, que leur lèvre mi-close,*
> *Souriante, semblait murmurer quelque chose . . .*

—Ils rêvent que, penchés sur leur petit bras rond,
Doux geste du réveil, ils avancent le front,
Et leur vague regard tout autour d'eux se pose.[3]

Is not this dreamed and happy awakening, contrasting so
sharply with the dark stretch of time preceding it, the first example in Rimbaud of those frequent moments in his work when
awakening is depicted as a sudden surge of being, beyond the
night, in a light that is usually that of dawn, like a phenomenon
wholly separated from the time preceding it? Most often, too, it
occurs as so sudden an event that it is not situated in time but
comparable, rather, to crying out.

Now, we know that the act of crying out—precisely because it
bears only the most accidental of relations to the context it rup-
tures, existing so to speak only within itself—is, of all the events
described to us by Rimbaud, the one that satisfies him most
deeply, the one bringing him the most intense joy. This is true to
such an extent that perfect happiness for him is something communicated to him directly, without extension or transition. It
comes mostly in the early morning, at night's end but before the
daylight has settled in: it is the crowing of the rooster.

Let us remember the text of *Une saison en enfer* which contains
one of the most beautiful of Rimbaldian songs, written in honor
of the "Gallic rooster":

> Happiness! Its tooth, sweet to death, warned me at
> the crowing of the cock,—*ad matutinum*, at the *Christus
> venit*—in the darkest cities:
>
> I have made the magic study
> Of happiness which no man evades.
> A salute to it each time
> The Gallic cock sings.
>
> *J'ai fait la magique étude*
> *Du bonheur qu'aucun n'élude*
> *Salut à lui, chaque fois*
> *Que chante le coq gaulois.*[4]

Need we emphasize that, for Rimbaud, the crowing, like the
surge of happiness in the two orphans, emerges out of obscurity,

3. "Les Etrennes des orphelins," 37 (13).   4. *Une saison en enfer,* 234 (201).

out of a type of anterior death, from which it emanates with the
piercing quality, the free torrent, of a crying out? But who utters
this cry? Who intervenes almost magically, suddenly, to shatter
the silence? Moreover, who discerns this cry, or hears it resonat-
ing within him? On the one hand, it is no doubt the poet who
awakens (or one of his protagonists). He cries out; he hears himself crying out. On the other hand, however, the crowing, like
the awakening of the orphans, is a phenomenon occurring on so
vast a scale that it seems to emanate from all of nature, such that
the orphans or the crowing rooster are not alone in opening their
eyes or making their song heard. That is what Rimbaud gives us
to understand in the poem "Les Etrennes des orphelins." Barely
has he spoken of the children's awakening when that particular
event reveals itself to be the awakening of all of nature:

> Nature awakens and is drunk with the rays of light . . .
> The earth, half-bare, happy to come alive again,
> Stirs with joy under the kisses of the sun.

> *La nature s'éveille et de rayons s'enivre.*
> *La terre demi-nue, heureuse de revivre,*
> *A des frissons de joie aux baisers du Soleil.*[5]

This renewal of the earth and world is so intense, so total, that
it cannot be simply the effect caused, in the minds of the two
children, by the return to consciousness. For Rimbaud, everything occurs as if the magic of waking and the transformational
act it engenders were first effected upon the whole of the cosmos,
before bearing upon the orphans' awakening. The orphans, tear-
ing themselves out of the night, come to merge their feelings with
the general movement of rebirth occurring everywhere in nature,
and moving the world—apparently instantaneously—from night
into day.

We see then that, beginning essentially with his first poem,
Rimbaud conceives of a possibility for remedying the deficiency
and unhappiness of certain awakenings of his own. He imagines
a miraculous process by which the ineffectuality of his past
awakenings is rectified. Not that the renewal of waking works
directly here on the two children; although the fund of sadness
that is theirs immediately gives way to joy, even to ecstasy. But

5. "Les Etrennes des orphelins," 38 (13).

the atmosphere of happiness which suddenly surrounds them does not stem from their own sensibilities; that atmosphere is manifest all around them beforehand, in the external world the children discern in their dream. What first awakens and transforms itself is not their internal state but, rather, nature, the earth, and the sun. The children are but the medium that allows for the revelation of cosmic upheavals. Thus their personal joy is preceded by, and perhaps even determined by, a phenomenon occurring on a far vaster scale. In opening their eyes to the daylight, the two children are obeying a movement that can be felt in the entire cosmos. Nature awakens first, and, because it does so, the children in turn emerge from sleep. In short, what Rimbaud wants irresistibly to suggest, is that the children's awakening (that is, the awakening of the young poet they represent) is preceded by the general awakening of nature. Everything is thus arranged such that, in the consciousness of the two orphans and in that of the poet who identifies with them, the act of waking—the sudden, intense, and full repossession of existence—appears as the direct consequence and direct extension of coming back to life, which nature has offered them for viewing. When I awake, whether my name is Rimbaud or any other name, I feel myself called to life, and to a consciousness of my own existence, by the intervention of a boundless energy, situated in nature and of divine essence. The phenomenon of waking is thus double: it may be perceived immediately, in the first instance, as the sudden manifestation of a creative force that emerges to summon back all that belongs to existence. Second, it may be seen as the no less sudden acquisition of consciousness, by which the awakening mind feels itself called to existence as a particular, through the workings of this same force.

When I awake, it means: I discover myself appearing or reappearing in existence—not by reason of a capacity for persistence in life, which would be inherent to my nature and thus a unique, indefinitely extended awakening. On the contrary, I awaken because of a superpersonal and perhaps also supernatural force that effects, (probably without interruption, and rather from moment to moment) the renewal of universal existence. In the same way, it effects within me, in moments always separate, the renewed perception of this existence. Through my renewed awakening, I thus gain the sense of a renewed world, and this by

79

the movement of a divine force endlessly intervening to create the world anew. The way I envision the world and myself is thus constituted by my awakenings (and those of nature)—that is, by a series of illuminations which, proceeding in the guise of successive discoveries of existence, are nevertheless separated by negative states: states of sleep, of nonbeing, or of absence.

Such is the experience of waking as it seems first to have appeared to the young Rimbaud; an experience not all of a piece, for it consists not in the discovery of a stable world, settled into existence for once and for all, but rather in acquisitions of consciousness, abruptly interrupted and abruptly repeated. It is from his first important poem, in other words, from his first explicit perception of existence, that Rimbaud decides to represent this existence as a thing always in danger of being severed. He never ceases representing it in this light. Existence will always remain for him a chain of poorly linked moments, noncausally connected, as distinct as possible each from the other, following upon each other independently, without fusing, as day follows night. For Rimbaud, there are awakenings, most often early morning ones. And there are dawns. These dawns, the first positive elements of continuance in Rimbaldian temporality, are strictly separated from each other by holes, and by gaps—that is, by those negative temporal elements which are, for Rimbaud, nights.

Thus it is against a background of night, but an interrupted night, that for Rimbaud the admirably positive reality of awakening is most often reconstituted, always manifesting itself with, so to speak, a terribly affirmative violence. It is the very act by which we escape mourning, death, the insufferable nothingness of darkness. It is thus the only moment in which we attain—but always temporarily and in the paradoxical form of an instantaneous eternity—happiness. Happiness is linked to the new day, to the birds starting to sing again, to eyes reopening. And happiness is not a lasting way of feeling one's existence. In Rimbaud, one does not live in a *state* of happiness. Hence, the "stirring" of joy, the "drunkenness," which, in the poem we have just considered,[6] equally affect the external world and the orphans who find themselves in it. Nature, on the one hand, and human conscious-

6. Ibid.

ness, on the other, pass through the world ineffably, without transition, from death to life. To awaken is to be restored to life. It is to feel oneself, inside an eternally isolated moment, being pulled out of nonbeing and animated (reanimated) instantaneously by a causal energy which, in Rimbaud—and there is no need to determine whether it works on the universality of nature or on the poet himself—most often bears the name of the *Sun*.

5

ORIGINAL AND UNIVERSAL cause of everything that is, and of everything that lives or is restored to life, the Rimbaldian sun is essentially a force of bestowal. From his first poems, Rimbaud identifies it with Venus, with Cybele, with the god of love. The Rimbaldian sun is thus not only a sacred or divine thing; it is more. Bearing a variety of names, it is divinity itself, exerting its creative work upon a world that depends on it in order to unfold into existence, or to reappear renewed at each moment of life. It is nothing less, therefore, than the creative God: unique, eternal, endlessly reapplying himself to his work; a God whose demiurgical power manifests itself not exactly in a continuous manner but, properly speaking, in a reiterated manner, through an activity which is at its most visible in the morning of each new day. Rimbaud thus more specifically associates the sun with that daily and grand new beginning of universal life, occurring at the start of each day. For him the sun is the great awakener, the one to whose call, from the depths of their sleep, all beings respond by gaining consciousness of self and of world. At the same time, the sun, by virtue of a rigorously immediate act, makes all that precedes it fade away—night, dream, the past—and imposes its animating power upon that which is born or reborn within the exclusive instant of the new day. Thus the sun's first act, its first creative act, initially manifests itself as negative and eliminative. It consists in making a clean slate of things. Before calling back into existence everything it touches, the light of dawn has the express purpose of evacuating everything that uselessly or harmfully precedes its apparition. In the dawn, as is described by Rimbaud, there is a nudity or regained virginity that cleanses objects of their ugliness, of their worn or sullied appearance, and restores them to their original state, without addition or alteration, in a universe strictly of the present.

It is perhaps in this perspective that one should read the following couplet in one of Rimbaud's poems:

> Under the arbors dawn evaporates
> The scent of the festive night.

> *Sous les bosquets l'aube évapore*
> *L'odeur du soir fêté;*[7]

and perhaps this sentence as well, taken from *Une saison en enfer:*

> At last, O happiness, O reason, I removed from the sky the blue that is black, and I lived like a spark of gold of pure light.[8]

The mind unwilling to tolerate the presence of any stain, even that of the azure, is prepared to accept only light alone, in its absolute purity. From that moment on, it participates without the shadow of a doubt or reservation in the illumination daily accomplished by the sun as it begins to light up the world. The Rimbaldian sun, then, is in no sense a transcendental power which, from the remote seat it occupies, confers a blessing upon the world from a distance—a blessing that does nothing to erase the existing separation between the divine nature of that creative star and the purely terrestrial character of the world thus favored. If Rimbaud, referring to himself (but perhaps also to any creature thus favored), dubs himself "sun-child,"[9] it is because he is intensely conscious of the consanguinity between him and the creative power to whose influx he submits. The connection he feels affecting him, the current he feels passing through him, the very breath that gives him life, far from appearing to originate from a wholly transcendental intervention, seem to him on the contrary to constitute a phenomenon whose fundamental immanence cannot be doubted. The first cognitive stance that can be distinguished in Rimbaud with respect to this giving God is not one

---

7. "Bonne pensée du matin," 155 (135).   8. *Une saison en enfer*, 232 (199).
9. *Illuminations*, "Vagabonds," 278 (233).

of respect, blindly felt for some withdrawn divinity with whom all connection is nearly impossible. It is quite the opposite: the recognition of a concrete relationship between a power hovering very near, and himself, the poet. Of this there can be no doubt: from the first, Rimbaud is a creature who feels himself to be in the closest—one might even say most intimate—contact with what directly affects him.

Not that this contact between himself and the illuminating, or creating, power implies the suppression of all distance between the two protagonists or, in the giving power, the absence of any innate superiority. In the act by which Rimbaud most often recognizes his fundamental debt to that which affords him light and life, there is an occasional sense of profound humility, even though it often includes its opposite—a feeling of arrogance. When, for example, in one of his first poems, "Les Effarés,"[10] he describes a group of children, cold and hungry, pressed against the red air-vent of a bakery, it never occurs to the poet to attenuate the magical superiority of a place that emanates warmth and life. The little beggars in question are "needy" beings because of the cold and hunger they feel, and their desire is wholly concentrated on receiving what they need. Hence their humility and dependence upon this "warm hole," which, says Rimbaud, "breathes out life." In the relationship thus described it is not difficult to discern an analogy, or rather the symbol, for another still more important relationship. The warm air emanating from the air vent, no doubt in successive puffs, represents quite clearly the mysterious transmission of the breath of life which (as happens in all the texts in which Rimbaud alludes to the hunger and thirst he suffers), pertains to a kind of help at times confusedly implored and, at others, confusedly received.

Another example of that concept, this time associated with the image of the sun, can be found in *Une saison en enfer,* from which the lines below are taken. The poet here describes himself at the very instant he receives the help he begs for. And that succor is so suddenly obtained that the fact of its being obtained is somehow disconcerting and unexpected:

> I have been shot in the heart by grace. Ah! I had not foreseen it![11]

10. "Les Effarés," 69–70 (49,51).   11. *Une saison en enfer,* 217 (181).

At the instant referred to here, the force that passes through the subject's soul has not been anticipated. It comes as a surprise, and we may suppose that the object of this phenomenon understands as yet neither its nature nor its scope. Thus it would perhaps be rash to take the word "grace" mentioned here in its strictly theological sense; that is, like help sent to a soul in need of salvation. It is not that this interpretation is false. But it simply implies, on the part of whoever might propose it, too explicit and defined a knowledge of the event in question, such as it is perceived at the moment it occurs. Indeed, it is most often in the most surprising fashion, in the greatest confusion, at the moment least expected—that creative or recreating grace, restoring spiritual existence to the soul receiving it, comes to touch that soul without imparting a precise knowledge of what is occurring. And yet at times this phenomenon takes place in response to an unarticulated request. Such is the case in another passage in *Une saison en enfer*. In contrast to what occurs in the preceding passage, here the intervention of the creative power is manifest in the form of an *answer*, immediately following the *offer* of himself made to that power by the being concerned.

Here is the text:

> I loved the desert, burnt orchards, musty shops, tepid drinks. I dragged myself through stinking alleys, and with my eyes closed, gave myself over to the sun, the god of fire.[12]

It matters little at this point whether the "god of fire" to whom the poet here offers his being is merely a random sunbeam or the supreme creative God, as he is imagined in any given religion. What is essential is that the poet is describing himself in the act that is the simplest and yet the most important to all life; the act by which, like the little "intimidated ones" (*effarés*), mentioned earlier in front of the red air vent, he *offers himself* to the infinitely beneficial effects of a sun, a light, and a warmth—that is, to a power that gives or transmits life. Furthermore, as we shall see, the aid here solicited has not only a reinvigorating property but also the power truly to transform the being upon which it works, *to give him another existence*, and thus magically to merge him, the

---

12. *Une saison en enfer*, "Alchimie du verbe," 231 (197).

petitioner, with the power at work within him. Indeed, several lines later Rimbaud gives us an unexpected image of this transmutation; an image deliberately chosen from among the most vulgar possible:

> Oh! the drunken gnat in the inn's urinal, in love with diuretic borage and dissolved by a sunbeam![13]

One cannot imagine a comparison—for it is one—more willfully unbecoming, introducing a grating disharmony between the two terms it considers in order ultimately to equate them. For through the miracle of a sunbeam touching a gnat, and in that fire that consumes it, the tiny creature seems to merge with the sun itself and to be an integral part of its splendor. The intervention of the sun causes the creature to renounce it own identity, to *become other*—that is, to become identical to the creator; a minuscule representation of God himself, living his divine life instantaneously. In one instant, the gnat transforms itself into God.

The deification of a creature by its assimilation into the very person of the creator—such is the phenomenon Rimbaud sees in the very act by which the creator effects his creative process. Such an act implies the simultaneous disintegration and a total recreation of life. The insignificance of the object so deified is of little importance. Equally unimportant is its baseness or, worse still, its vile appearance. For this object, as we have seen, may be a gnat in a public urinal. It may also be excrement, filth: "The sovereign sun sank into shit,"[14] we read in a variant of "Alchimie du verbe." This line should be taken literally as a description of the creative mind's descent into matter, and as the alchemical metamorphosis it effects in the latter, by dint of which filth is changed into a divine substance.

The metamorphosis in question thus implies the descent of the creative principle—that is, the action by which that principle lowers itself into the realm of nature. Even in his early poems, Rimbaud intuited the spirit's great sliding descent, bringing to the world below what initially exists only far above it. In Rimbaud's early works we often encounter the image of a divinity pouring out its power over a world stretching out far below it. Thus, in "Soleil et chair":

13. Ibid.   14. 335.

The Sun, hearth of tenderness and life,
Pours burning love over the delighted earth.

Le soleil, le foyer de tendresse et de vie,
Verse l'amour brûlant à la terre ravie.[15]

A few lines later, Rimbaud returns to the same word and writes:

I miss the time of great Cybele . . .
Her two breasts poured into the immense depths
The pure stream of infinite life.

Je regrette les temps de la grande Cybèle . . .
Son double sein versait dans les immensités
Le pur ruissellement de la vie infinie.[16]

The creative power that Rimbaud places above creation thus innundates creation, through a *stream of blessings;* blessings that are dispersed in the double immensity of time and space. There is a multiplicity of divine interventions, endlessly splitting themselves into the vastness of the universe, injecting into it everywhere an inexhaustible plurality of forms. We shall have occasion to discuss this last phenomenon in another chapter, which will be devoted to the role of the *number* in Rimbaud's work. Let me for the present merely emphasize that there can be no *descent* nor distribution in the Rimbaldian universe without the presence of a passive element corresponding to the active.

The one giving (or pouring out), has a counterpart in the one who receives. Between these two beings, one the giver, the other the receiver, there is necessarily a great difference, at least at the outset. As we have seen, it is with humility that the little "effarés" receive what they are offered. Moreover, it is the consciousness of what they lack that brings them to the discovery that they are in contact with abundance. Regardless of the occasional proximity to be seen in Rimbaud between the donating power and the receptive, created being, the contrast immediately erupting in the poet's work between the first and the second of these cannot be overemphasized. It is the contrast between strength and weakness, plenty and want, the act of giving and the act—if it is one—of receiving. In Rimbaud, however, the marks of weakness and of want are never definitive. All that can be said is that episodically, fleetingly, they nevertheless play an

15. "Soleil et chair," 40 (27).   16. Ibid.

essential part in the relationship the poet establishes between supernature and his own nature. But let me hasten to add, while there is still time—for in Rimbaud all stages are ablaze and experienced at top speed—that for him there is an instant, one immediately left behind, in which he places himself of his own volition in the position proper to the created being in the presence of his creator, that is, in the position of humbly receiving. Rimbaud *feels* with extraordinary intensity (his entire opus proves it) this gift granted him of each moment of existence. He feels it *first* as coming from elsewhere and from above; as having as its origin a source infinitely superior to him—let us say it: a *divine source.* Seen from this point of view, and remaining within the extremely narrow confines of that point of view—as did, for example, Claudel—the Rimbaldian experience could hardly be more authentically Christian. It is the experience of one who accepts— with all the intensity of feeling that this miracle inspires, with a sense of the deepest gratitude—the gift of existence and all its riches, conferred by the great Other: "Let us welcome," he writes one day, "all the influxes of vigor and real tenderness."[17]

What is received—and, it would appear, with what gratitude!—is not an objective gift, a type of present, a material thing transmitted from one person to another. It is rather a current of life which, generated from a first being called the giver, continues and is extended to another person, called the receiver. One transmits to the other a power that originally was within him alone. Here the living being does not merely see itself receiving some supplementary advantage or external adjunct; it finds itself, through the activity of this influx or current passing through it, to a certain extent *becoming* what it receives, and, consequently, it experiences itself as being transformed (at least, within the limits imposed by its nature) into the very being by whose influx it has been penetrated. If, in Rimbaud's eyes, the sun gives off a light that crosses intermediate space in order to come and enlighten him, he himself feels changed in turn into an interior sun, so that the ego, which is the depository of this light, becomes a light in its own right, and the illuminating power communicated to it truly becomes its own. "I lived," writes Rimbaud, "like a spark of gold of pure light."[18] For him, the spark of gold is thus not only a

17. *Une saison en enfer,* "Adieu," 241 (209).   18. Ibid., "Faim," 232 (199).

reflection but the new hearth where the emanated light is re-kindled. Thus the concept of the relation between illuminator and illuminated, between creator and created, is profoundly modified. The recipient's ego no longer shows the complete humility his state had initially inspired. No one is less likely to be confused with an inferior or dependent creature than this new god who emerges from man when he feels within him the outpouring of the "influx of vigor and real tenderness." This influx, emanating from a God, has as its goal the remaking of a god. The creator, extending his influx to his creature, makes him into a new creator. In Rimbaud's spiritual history, then, nothing is more important than the mental act by which he ascertains, accepts, and uses from within himself this incredible transferral of creative power. It is a power that makes him see himself as a creator who is, if not equal to, at least second to God. This conviction motivates a metamorphosis of infinite depth to operate within the poet; a metamorphosis of such daring that its equivalent is to be found only in the most infamous of heresies. What Rimbaud believes he recognizes in himself is something almost identical to the direct consanguinity between Father and Son. Rimbaud identifies with God or, at least, grants himself the privilege of divine powers. Creation's creature becomes the creator.

6

"Let us welcome," Rimbaud had written, "all the influxes of vigor and real tenderness." Let us welcome the *influxes*. From the outset, one wonders what kind of influxes these are and how they manifest themselves in the individual who feels their advent. When does the influx of vigor and tenderness occur? How is that which comes from the outside received within the being experiencing its activity? Finally, what is the nature of this influx, at least initially? If one returns to Rimbaud's early texts and to the impression they make on the reader, there is no doubt that for Rimbaud the influx of vigor and tenderness appears from the first as belonging to the realm of the senses.

Such is the case in the poem entitled, precisely, "Sensation":

In the blue summer evenings, I will go along the paths,
And walk over the short grass, as I am pricked by the
wheat:
Daydreaming I will feel the coolness on my feet.
I will let the wind bathe my bare head.

Par les soirs bleus d'été, j'irai dans les sentiers,
Picoté par les blés, fouler l'herbe menue:
Rêveur, j'en sentirai la fraîcheur à mes pieds.
Je laisserai le vent baigner ma tête nue.[19]

Let us not be fooled, in reading this quatrain, by the tense of
the verbs. Even if the sensory experience of which the poet
speaks here is somehow anticipated by the mind and thus projected into the future, that experience is in fact so intense and so
fresh that it is beyond any doubt experienced in the present.
What the poet feels, mentally if not physically, is an experience
within the present.

But it is also an experience of external reality. The poet is attentive, not only to what he will soon feel in time, but also to what he
will soon feel in space. The poem situates the walker in a place in
the countryside, where the barbed heads of wheat prick him,
where the grass is fresh, where the wind bathes his head as he
wanders by. Contact between him and the place through which
he wanders is thus repeated three times. The place shares an
intimacy with the person walking through it, who himself feels
the bond he shares with it in three different but contiguous ways.
The resulting impression is that of an extreme proximity between
things determining the sensations experienced (the wheat, grass,
and wind) and the subject undergoing these sensations. Between
outside and inside, objects and subject, contact could be no
closer. And of all the senses, the one dominating the realization
of these connections is that which emphasizes the proximity
most successfully, overtly, concretely. That sense, obviously, is
touch.

The sense of touch is perhaps the primary of all our senses.
First in chronology, if not in importance, it is the most authentically primitive. It is probably the sense which, above all others,
is best adapted to reveal instantly to us the nature of the environ-
ment in which we find ourselves; the sense that brings us the

19. "Sensation," 39 (17).

most immediate information about the outside. It is through the sense of touch that we are able, by merely walking or coming into contact with things, immediately to recognize the existence of a world of objects. Touching then plays an important role, a role both indispensable and fundamental in our discovery of objective reality.

And yet is this what Rimbaud's poem reveals to us? The existence in-itself (*en soi*) of the objective world, which exists of itself, alone, there on the outside, can only leave him utterly indifferent. What counts for him in his relation to the world is the way in which this relation reveals him to be himself in his own eyes. Ultimately, neither the wheatfield he crosses, nor the freshness of the grass, nor the racing wind bear any special significance for him. What matters to him, what captures his attention, is the pricking, the personal sensation of freshness, and a way of feeling his face caressed by the wind.

In other words, the first and most essential data conveyed by the sensations in question here all refer back to the poet's body. For Rimbaud, to multiply one's experiences in the external world is to have a revelation of one's own body, a revelation which, if not exclusive, certainly remains preeminent—and this by virtue of the contact he has with the external world. That world, in its pure objectivity, does not of course reveal itself to the poet; or, if it does, it is by means of revelations which, to the extent that they affect external agents, remain only secondary, fortuitous, and incomplete. The only phenomenon to impress the walker and, we may consequently assume, the poet as well, is the role played by consciousness of self (termed kinesthesic) in the mind of that individual. For the person who grants it a naive and thus all the more acute attention, the body—especially the body in motion—reveals itself to be an inexhaustible source of exclusively intimate information concerning the living being one is. The consciousness of self one possesses at the moment one yields, in walking or in any other activity, to the most direct and freshest of sensations, is then no different from the consciousness occasionally experienced in bed at the moment of *awakening*. In both cases there is a rediscovery of the self—not that type of worn familiarity one has with one's own person in the ordinary course of existence, but a contact with the self that is absolutely new and, therefore, absolutely intense as well.

For Rimbaud, to feel is to feel *oneself*. As sudden, even as violent, as certain physical contacts may be for him, they are always seen through a consciousness of self that never loses its ludicity. Sensation is joined by a perceptive mode of thinking, which operates not only on the object at hand but on the perceiving subject as well. This feature is to be found nearly everywhere in Rimbaud's work. It may be, for example, the consciousness of self experienced by the adolescent when stealing furtive glances at the young girls sitting next to him while a military band plays in the great square of Mézières:

> I do not say a word: I keep looking
> At the flesh of their white necks embroidered with stray locks . . .
> Burning with fine fevers, I reconstruct the bodies . . .
> And feel the kisses which come to my lips.

> *Je ne dis pas un mot: je regarde toujours*
> *La chair de leurs cous blancs brodés de mèches folles . . .*
> *Je reconstruis les corps, brûlé de belles fièvres . . .*
> *Et je sens les baisers qui me viennent aux lèvres.*[20]

This consciousness of one's own body through the perception of the body of others is too common a phenomenon to merit further discussion. But it can be found again in other guises. For example, in the sense of self acquired by the child being deloused:

> The child feels, according to the slowness of the caresses,
> Surging in him and dying continuously a desire to cry.

> *L'enfant se sent, selon la lenteur des caresses,*
> *Sourdre et mourir sans cesse un désir de pleurer.*[21]

And in still another passage:

> —We are overcome by it all.
> The sap is champagne and goes to our head . . .
> We talked a lot and feel a kiss on our lips
> Trembling there like a small insect.

20. "A la musique," 60 (494; I have retranslated the last line of this poem in order to make Poulet's point.—Trans.).
21. "Les Chercheuses de poux," 127 (93).

—*On se laisse griser.*
La sève est du champagne et vous monte à la tête. . .
On divague; on se sent aux lèvres un baiser
Qui palpite là, comme une petite bête.[22]

Or again these words from the poet about those he calls the "Intimidated":

They feel so renewed with life . . .
    That they are all there
Gluing their small pink snouts
To the grating.

Ils se ressentent si bien vivre . . .
    Qu'ils sont là tous
Collant leurs petits museaux roses
Au treillage.[23]

What seems to emerge from all these texts is that sensory experience—and, of course, this includes all sexual experience—implies, for Rimbaud, not only the presence of pure sensation (which exists without reflection), but also, especially, a frequently very vivid perception of himself becoming aware of that sensation. For him, then, this perception tends to be deeply interiorized. Rimbaud most often sees it as an influence which, emanating from the outside, extends into him; first, to affect his senses, but also to modify his very being. To feel is to feel one*self;* that is, to perceive the change brought about in us by the sensory event as a phenomenon which captures our attention. Another example of this is to be found in the particular quality that aural sensations acquire for Rimbaud when he contemplates the glittering stars:

. . . I listened to them, seated on the side of the road,
In those good September evenings when I felt drops
Of dew on my brow, like a strong wine.

. . . je les écoutais, assis au bord des routes,
ces bons soirs de septembre où je sentais des gouttes
De rosée à mon front, comme un vin de vigueur.[24]

22. "Roman," 71 (53).   23. "Les Effarés," 70 (51).
24. "Ma Bohème," 81 (63).

This influx—the influx of vigor—seems to be caused by what Rimbaud calls the rustling [*frou-frou*] activity of the distant stars. This activity suggests the journey their light must complete in order to reach the contemplator. He perceives simultaneously the phenomenon and himself being conscious of the length of their completed trek. This self-displacing sensation is so powerful that it can be felt even at the end of a long period of travel.

For Rimbaud, this is particularly true of certain sensations that are by nature more nomadic than others, and which come to assault the spectator from afar:

> The good orchards with blue grass,
>> And twisted apple trees!
> How you smell a league off
>> Their strong perfume!

> *Les bons vergers à l'herbe bleue,*
>> *Aux pommiers tors!*
> *Comme on les sent toute une lieue*
>> *Leurs parfums forts!*[25]

More often for Rimbaud, however, odor is not to be captured within the movement that spreads it, as it were, excentrically into space. In this, as in several other more important points, Rimbaud differs profoundly from Baudelaire, for whom the propagation of scent is an occasion granted the poet to accompany the perfume on its path, thus letting himself be carried along into the expanses of space. For Rimbaud, on the contrary, the manifestation of odor seems, for the subject experiencing it, the opportunity of being closely tied to that odor in the place where it exerts its influence on him. Odor is thus situated within the restricted limits of the place from which it emanates and touches the nostrils of its perceiver. Moreover, the strength of an odor seems for Rimbaud to be in proportion to the often fetid character of places from which it springs:

> It will smell of the stable, full
>> Of warm manure.

> *Ca sentira l'étable, pleine*
>> *De fumiers chauds.*[26]

---

25. "Les Réparties de Nina," 67 (45).   26. Ibid.

> He was bent
> On shutting himself up in the coolness of the outhouse:
> There he meditated, peacefully, opening his nostrils.

> *Il était entêté*
> *A se renfermer dans la fraîcheur des latrines:*
> *Il pensait là, tranquille et livrant ses narines.*[27]

It goes without saying that in Rimbaud's work the experience is usually all the more intense when it violates the rules of good taste. But there is more. What is called a bad smell, or stench, has (to use the poet's own term) more "vigor" and thus more "influx" than any other. The power of the experience can be better perceived, even if the shock of the sensation has the frequent result, as Stendhal noted, of preventing us from discerning its nuances.

Everything is then arranged according to a clearly delineated relation between two ways of feeling (and even of speaking), each as distinct as possible from the other. On the one hand, there is a surging source of sensations—so vivid, so spontaneous, and at times even so violent that it brutally invades the senses of the one it affects. On the other hand, there is the ego, which finds itself thus assaulted. The subject discovers himself to be split in two. First, there is inside him—invading him, imposing itself upon him, remolding his person—an influx of energy that dizzies him, jostles him, takes hold of him, and prevents him from experiencing anything else. But there is also a dazed consciousness, still reeling from the shock, unable to feel or think of anything else, and hence in danger of losing all personal traits, all individual characteristics.

This absence of personality is frequently expressed by the poet, for example, in the use he makes of the indefinite pronoun "one." "One is overcome by it all . . ."[28] "One talks a lot, and feels a kiss on one's lips . . ."[29] "One feels in opened things the quivering of flesh."[30] *One* replaces *I*, and reveals through this substitution a characteristic weakening of the sense of self in a mind more disposed toward submission than reaction. This hab-

27. "Les Poètes de sept ans," 95 (77).
28. "Roman," 71 (53; in this and the following two notes, I have replaced Fowlie's "we" or "you" with "one," for obvious reasons.—Trans).
29. Ibid.   30. "Le Réparties de Nina," 64 (41).

it, a sporadic one in Rimbaud, results not necessarily in the total
suppression of the individual but, rather, in his reduction to a
simple *one*. Semianonymous, almost neuter, essentially passive,
this is an individual who is generally content to receive with
docility the given impulse. Whether the force of creativity, in
such sharp relief as it is with Rimbaud, manifests itself in the form
of a creative divinity or, more humbly, in the phenomenon of
sensory existence, the result is the same. It tends to create within
the individual experiencing it a doubling of being, and a profound depersonalization.

7

THERE IS IN RIMBAUD, then, a certain desire to be a *one*, that is, to
submit to the influence given him to experience. Nevertheless,
an opposing tendency in him is clearly distinguishable from the
start: a tendency that consists in making the ego not the passive
product of an external creative activity but the internal principle
of that activity. A creating ego, not a created one—this is the ideal
Rimbaud sets for himself from the beginning of his poetic career.
This creating ego appears in the long poem "Le Forgeron," in
which a man of the people lectures the king of France in declamatory tones. If we set aside the aggressively political aspect of this
poem, we will not be wrong in seeing in this work the first manifestation in Rimbaud of what we may call the ego-creator. For the
blacksmith, a powerful teacher, essentially presents himself as
the capable tamer of objects and living things:

> We are
> For the great new times when men will want to know,
> When Man will forge from morning to night,
> A hunter of great effects, hunter of great causes,
> When, slowly victorious, he will tame things,
> And mount everything as one mounts a horse.

> *Nous sommes*
> *Pour les grands temps nouveaux où l'on voudra savoir,*
> *Où l'Homme forgera du matin jusqu'au soir,*
> *Chasseur des grands effets, chasseur des grandes causes,*

Où, lentement vainqueur, il domptera les choses
Et montera sur Tout, comme sur un cheval![31]

In the manner of much of Hugo's verse which, in fact, these lines vaguely resemble), what is clearly affirmed in the text above is the fact that man, master of his destiny, freely asserts his will upon the world of things. The poem's tone is clearly political and revolutionary. But this aspect is perhaps less important than the intention the poem reveals of "taming things," that is, of asserting oneself as a controlling and creating principle in the presence of objects. In short, it is not an overstatement to claim that in this text the Rimbaldian man behaves, as the poet conceives of him, not only as a revolutionary but as a type of demiurge of Promethean proportions.

"The poet," writes Rimbaud in a famous letter, "is truly the thief of fire."[32] It is he who substitues himself for the legitimate or initial creator, he who assumes His position, taking upon himself the task that had been His. He is an "inventor," to employ the term Rimbaud will apply to himself. He is an inventor, certainly—but in Rimbaldian language this term does not so much mean "one who finds" as someone who imposes a new manner of being, a recreation, upon what he finds.

To invent, for Rimbaud, is thus to create or, better still, to recreate.

But what is recreated in this way?

First and foremost, they are very general things: life, love, nature, humanity itself.

"Does he perhaps have secrets for changing life?" Rimbaud has Verlaine ask, presumbaly speaking of Rimbaud.[33]

"I have created all celebrations," Rimbaud says this time in his own voice, "all triumphs, all dramas. I have tried to invent new flowers, new stars, new flesh, new tongues." And he adds, "I believed I had acquired supernatural powers."[34]

It becomes clear then, if all the words used by the poet are compared, that to change life does not merely mean to replace it by a slightly different version from one before. It means, rather, to replace wholly, in its entirety and thus in the originality and

31. "Le Forgeron," 55–56 (23).
32. "Lettre à Demeny," 15 May 1871, 347 (309).
33. *Une saison en enfer*, 225 (189)   34. Ibid., "Adieu," 240 (207).

multiplicity of the aspects it presents—the existence of everything that is, with *another form of existence.* And this is to be done in
so radical a manner that the verb *to change* seems inadequate for
expressing such a metamorphosis, so that to give a better idea of
it one should resort to such words as "invent," "create," "the
use of supernatural powers."

In a word, the will to change here reveals itself to be so vast and
so profound, that it allows nothing that existed previously to
survive. It insists upon an integral renewal. This renewal is envi-
sioned to be the most general conceivable. It applies, without
differentiation, to everything encountered on the outside:
flowers, trees, the heavens, the earth, and the oceans. The result
is that the one who wants total change assumes an obligation that
becomes almost inconceivable. It consists, on the one hand, in
destroying, or in considering as destroyed or nonexistent, all the
realities of external life (flowers, trees, the heavens, earth, and
flesh), all forms of matter; and, on the other hand, in establishing, within the immense vacuum they leave in the wake of their
disappearance, absolutely unprecedented forms of the same objects they replace.

Obviously, a transformation of this sort—and this is the only
restriction to which the exigencies of such an undertaking will
admit—need not require changes that are, strictly speaking, material. Everything, indeed, occurs as if matter had never existed,
or had in no sense a real existence. The transformation in question here does not therefore imply an authentic destruction of
matter, and recognizes the objective, unaltered continuation of
all objects reputedly material. Rimbaud's project of universal recreation, then, stops here. Assuredly, it respects nothing. It denies what exists. It even denies the existence of a superior being,
of the real creator of the world. It replaces Him—beneficially,
from its perspective—with the presence and activity of the Promethean worker, who is the poet. Nevertheless—and this point
merits emphasis—in leaving matter untouched, in leaving it as is,
and in guarding against imposing a destiny upon it, Rimbaud in
one sense lets everything that is excluded from his internal activity subsist on the outside.

It remains for us to examine this internal activity. Needless to
say, Rimbaud wants it so radically renewed that it will resemble
real existence as little as possible. It will exist of its own, and not

by reason of its resemblance or contiguity to an actual world, from which it is quite clearly dissociated. In short, by letting the outside world subsist such as it really is (indeed, unable to do otherwise), but by concomitantly acting as if it did not exist, Rimbaud assigns himself a task that is not limited (it remains infinite) but, rather, *defined;* a task that consists in behaving as if the only things that could occupy his thought and guide his actions were dependent, ultimately, upon his imagination alone.

Henceforth, Rimbaud's project takes a very precise direction. It presents itself as an exclusively imaginary project, unfolding entirely from within the limits of the inventor's mental life; that is, within himself. No doubt this interior can be somehow furnished at will, as Rimbaud writes, with all sorts of new objects. Thus the new flowers, new stars, new flesh of which the poet speaks in a text cited earlier are certainly objects there, but objects of a special kind, given that, created as they were by the inventive power of the poet, and graced by him with all the original attributes of an external existence, they nevertheless can be situated only within the interior of creative thought itself. The same holds true for all objects imagined, and even for the space they occupy in the interior of the mind that imagines them, such that the Rimbaldian creative act, creating an infinity of purely mental objects, simultaneously creates a mental space for receiving them—a space equally different from external space. Referring to himself, but also to all poets or "seers" capable of accomplishing this magic act, Rimbaud calls them (and himself with them) "master jugglers"[35] and gives us to understand that they "transform place" (as they do people) through a procedure Rimbaud calls a "magnetic comedy."[36] According to these rules, the interior space Rimbaud envisions appears as an imagined space, a space thus humanly structured (no different from the way architects build one). And yet it goes without saying that it is not to be confused with real, external space, in the sense that it is not a *given* space (given perhaps by the creator, who is, of them all, first in rank and time—that is, God). As the creator of his own space, man no longer situates himself in a space he receives and accepts. On the contrary, the poet becomes the giver of his own space; he is first the giver, since he integrally invents the places in which he decid-

---

35. *Illuminations,* "Parade," 261 (225).   36. Ibid.

es imaginatively to reside; and yet he is also, secondly, the one to whom it *is given* to see himself situated at the interior of his own space. Consequently, at once creator and creature, on the one hand man is the creator of his space and, on the other, he must submit to behaving within that space as if it had been given him.

The same ambiguity is to be found in the realm of Rimbaldian time. For on the one hand (once again), in the manner of God himself, the Rimbaldian poet will create the time in which he lives, that is, separately invent as it were each moment of his life. He no longer feels himself to be living in *God's time;* in other words, in the uninterrupted continuity of terrestrial life as it is sustained by divine will (or by the laws governing matter). Rather, he feels himself living in a time perpetually renewed by his own intervention. He lives from moment to moment, inventing each of them in turn. In a sense, then, as we shall see more fully below, he is the author of each moment in his life. He gives himself the joy of existing. But he also sees this joy conferred upon him by his own hand. At once active and passive, he is both the one who grants himself existence, and the one receiving it. He is, so to speak, both *exister* and *existee,* just as he is the one who gives himself a space in which to live and the one who receives the ability to reside within it by his own leave.

Such a dichotomy would be inconceivable within the realm of divinity. It seems logical to us to conceive of the existence of God as identical to his own duration (which is eternity), and of space, which is his, as identical to his immensity. But on the human level the *creator* and the *created,* the *continuer* [*durant*] and the *continued* [*duré*], the *extending power* and the *capacity-to-be-extended* are not united in the same person. Man creates neither his time nor his space; he is content to receive them. The same is not true for Rimbaud. He is both creator and creature; the one who gives himself a certain way to continue and the one who accepts such continuance.

Inventor of his own time, of his own space, Rimbaud also ineluctably forces himself to invent his own behavior in time and space. If he loves, he loves in two ways: he doubtless submits to his love, but he must also invent it. "I am an inventor . . . who found something resembling the key of love."[37] This key is per-

---

37. *Illuminations,* "Vies," 264 (229).

haps the fact that the lover, as the active one, does not distinguish himself from the lover who is passive. Within love, too, for Rimbaud, creation and reception are intertwined.

And in speech. Rimbaud prided himself "on inventing a poetic language accessible some day to all the senses."[38] He therefore does not merely invent a language; he must direct it to an interlocutor who understands it, who will respond to it, and who, in that sense, is someone like him. He is then both the speaker and the one spoken to. Such is the invariable dialectic to which all Rimbaldian creation must submit. It assumes a creator who is the same person as his creature. It is simultaneously in the same movement, in the same time, in the same place and in the same being, that for Rimbaud the magical activity of the creator and the passivity of the created being meet and merge. As different as these two persons may be (for Rimbaud, unlike Mallarmé, does not strive to be mirrored in the hyperbolic self-image he would engender—on the contrary), the creating being and the one created must resemble each other on one level: they exist in the most intimate of associations, like a symbiotic or androgynous being. Thus it is that, from within such a dyad, one can say of the other (as Verlaine is made to say in *Une saison en enfer* in speaking of Rimbaud), "I will wake up, and laws and customs will have changed—thanks to his magical power."[39] A magical power in Rimbaud that might have awakened Verlaine? No doubt. But even more certain is Rimbaud's magical power, which, with or without the mediation of Verlaine, awakens Rimbaud himself. The creator awakens one other than himself, one who is nevertheless he. In such a text we rediscover the word *awaken,* which served as the point of departure for this essay. And now we learn something new about the Rimbaldian awakening: that this type of emerging consciousness of self, always erupting like an event without precedent in the mind of whoever experiences it, is never so intense, so rich, so magical, as when are joined to it and merged with it the intoxication of creating and the joy of being created, perceived as the same act. In Rimbaud, then, consciousness of self is at once single and double.

38. *Une saison en enfer,* "Alchimie du verbe," 228 (193).
39. Ibid., "Délires," 226 (191).

8

IN RIMBAUD, THEN, we frequently see a doubled consciousness of self. The same is in fact true for him with regard to the concept of cause. At times, Rimbaud experiences himself as self-created,— that is, as *causing* his own existence. In this case, as we shall see at greater length below, he manifests himself in the guise of a determining power, free to create itself, as it is to create anything it pleases. "I am a master of hallucinations," he writes in *Une saison en enfer*.[40] At other times, by contrast, he sees himself as the direct result of this determining action. Then, far from feeling free, he has the sensation of being determined by an unspecified demiurgic power, to whose actions he submits. In this second case, experimenting with what he undergoes, Rimbaud arrives at a type of *cogito* that is diametrically opposed to that of Descartes. He transcribes it as follows:

> It is wrong to say: I think. One ought to say: *one* thinks me.[41]

Instead of thinking himself in the naked simplicity of his thinking activity, here, in this particular version of consciousness of self, we have Rimbaud perceiving himself as being thought—that is, as the result of a mental activity so impersonal that it is impossible to designate it other than by the indefinite pronoun: *One* thinks me! In fact, this amounts to saying (saying *to oneself*): I am, I do not doubt my existence; nor do I doubt that it is personal, or that the way in which I apprehend it is not equally personal. I am, and feel myself to be, living. But this being that I am and of which I am conscious, is dependent upon a power I cannot reasonably attibute to myself. My effort to think myself can only lead me to situate, somewhere back of me, a determining power of which I am the passive subject and about which I am at a loss to speak.

In short, this first *cogito* of Rimbaud's leads to a presentation of the ego as reflecting upon itself, like a being whose existence is

---

40. Ibid., "Nuit de l'enfer," 221 (185).
41. "Lettre à Izambard," 13 May 1871, 345 (303; again, here the pronoun has been changed from Fowlie's "people" to "one."—Trans.).

suspended by the power of a creating, suprapersonal thought, one impossible for the ego to fathom.

But there is a second Rimbaldian *cogito*, diametrically opposed to the first. It is the one capable of fashioning a being which, instead of considering itself as "thought" or as "created," would consider itself, on the contrary, as thinking itself and, by the same token, creating itself. We have seen that, in what we may term Rimbaud's fundamental point of departure, the conscious ego appears to be inventing itself. The result was that, for the poet of the *Illuminations*, there were precisely two ways of considering his ego (and his thought): either as *received* or, on the contrary, as *given*. Inevitably, if the Rimbaldian being puts himself in the position of one who perceives himself as receiving life, he situates himself in a perspective opposite to that in which he sees himself as its giver.

This new position necessarily implies a very different sort of *cogito*. In the first instance I must say to myself: *One thinks me (On me pense)*. In the second instance I am constrained to say to myself something essentially like this; It is I who think and who, in thinking, engender a being who is still myself.

This should be, for Rimbaud, the conclusion of a consciousness-of-self theory. It would result in the perfect opposition of two kinds of consciousnesses-of-self, mutually antipodal, but presupposing a common principle: that the thinking (or creating) ego and the thought (or created) ego would not ultimately differ in character.

But this is not the case at all. From Rimbaud's perspective there is no necessary identification, or even similarity, between the two egos. By way of a new and perhaps even more surprising paradox than the one according to which the ego thinks itself and creates itself, Rimbaud acknowledges, and even upholds (and with such vigor that one cannot but help seeing here the culminating and therefore most audacious aspect of his thinking) the notion that the creating and thinking ego can grant itself *another* ego, an ego radically different from the one it initially possessed: *I is another [Je est un autre]*.

So Rimbaud affirms the great principle of the ego's alterity in relation to itself. This signifies: I can think myself other than I am or was. Moreover, and infinitely more serious: I can create (or recreate) myself other than I was.

But this other ego, stranger to me but nonetheless emerging from my creative thought—am I not able to recognize it as mine, as identical to me? Here the answer can only be wholly negative. I can be "present at this birth of my thought,"[42] I can be aware that its emergence into the light of day depends entirely upon me; but the dissimilarity between the two egos is so great that no bridge can be erected between the ego that is the creative power and the other ego, born of me, which is the created ego. The gap between them is absolute. It is so great that between the creating ego and the other, created ego I can establish no bond—save the fact, perhaps inexplicable, that, in a sense, as the creating ego I must recognize myself as the author of the created being who can claim, like me, to be myself. The result is that Rimbaud, in the situation he engenders through the personal excercise of his creative power, finds himself in the position of a hen hatching a duck egg. He endlessly gives birth to another him, who is concomitantly not he at all. To use his own words, he is "the wood which finds itself [to be] a violin,"[43] "the brass [that] wakes up a trumpet."[44]

The wood is not the real cause of the violin, any more than the brass is the real cause of the trumpet. And yet, they are its incidental cause (*cause occasionelle*).

But incidental causes, as we know, are not real causes; they are only "incidents" by means of which certain effects are produced. One cannot then claim that, if "the brass wakes up a trumpet," the brass has had a real part in the appearance of this phenomenon: "it is not its fault."[45] The same holds true for the wood that discovers itself to be a violin. This metamorphosis is not, ultimately, the wood's doing, since there is no common gauge between the wood and the violin. What Rimbaud means is that there can be no bond whatever between the creating ego and that other, created ego. All that can be said is that one takes the place of the other. But this succession involves no paternity, no filiation, no connection between cause and effect, no continuity in time or space. The most to be said is that, for Rimbaud, one "draws a stroke of the bow" and the other is "the symphony

42. "Lettre à Demeny," 15 May 1871, 345 (305).
43. "Lettre à Izambard," 13 May 1871, 344 (305).
44. "Lettre à Demeny," 15 May 1871, 345 (305).   45. Ibid.

[that] makes it stir in the depths, or comes on to the stage in a leap."[46]

But whether the symphony stirs or leaps, one thing only is certain. Its leaping, its stirring, constitute an action that bears no evident relation to anything preceding it. It is a little like what André Gide was later to call the *acte gratuit*, or, better put, it is *arbitrary*. The total alterity of the second *I* from the first *I* has as its inevitable consequence the novelty—itself total—of this second *I*. I who become conscious of myself in the absence of all connection with a preceding I—I am ignorant of, I reject, or I deny any state that antedates my thought. I do not admit of being bound by any previous action or conception whatever, of which I might be the author. My consciousness of self begins only with me, and this *me* is one that awakens into existence for the first time. Thus the dialectic of consciousness and alterity in Rimbaud culminates in the affirmation of the *virginity* of existence's every moment. I, Rimbaud, I live, think, create (and am created) for the first time with every moment. And my newness includes the newness of everything surrounding me, of everything revealed to me or emanating from me. I am a new being in a new universe.

9

IN HIS INTENSE DESIRE to be new, to be exempted or liberated at every moment from everything that preceded this very newness, Rimbaud was confronted with a virtually unsolvable problem.

What is new never remains so. It can never be said to exist, for, from the moment it is spoken of, it no longer exists as new, it is limited to having been so. There can be no such thing as old new; there can only be the perpetual reinvention of a "new new," which itself only lasts in the extraordinarily brief time it is a momentary novelty. In contrast to Gide, Rimbaud did not always understand the law, rigid as it is, that condemns all that is new to never lasting, nor having lasted.

It is thus that in "Soleil et chair"—which is, as we know, one of

46. Ibid.

his earliest poems—Rimbaud takes himself back to former times when love was engendered by the gods, and thus dreams of his renewal in a future epoque:

> O splendor of flesh! O ideal splendor!
> O renewal of love, triumphal dawn
> When, prostrating Gods and Heroes at their feet,
> White Callipyge and little Eros,
> Covered with the snow of roses,
> Will lightly touch women and flowers full-blown under
>   their beautiful feet!

> *O splendeur de la chair! ô splendeur idéale!*
> *O renouveau d'amour, aurore triomphale*
> *Où, courbant à leurs pieds les Dieux et les Héros,*
> *Kallipyge la blanche et le petit Eros*
> *Effleureront, couverts de la neige des roses,*
> *Les femmes et les fleurs sous leurs beaux pieds écloses!*[47]

On the one hand, there is already something clearly very Rimbaldian about this poem: the coincidence of the event referred to with the very moment in which the poet makes it happen. This "renewal of love" sung by the poet merges at his will with a particular time which is both the general beginning of all eras, and the beginning of each day. The birth of love occurs in a "triumphal dawn"; a dawn once again reminiscent of the fundamental association Rimbaud makes between the theme of waking and that of being born (or reborn) into life.

On the other hand, this birth is relegated to the past as a mythic event by Rimbaud. It is thus what we have called "old new." The poet must renew it—that is, transpose it into another time—and he does this, so to speak, with a leap, by passing over the intervening ages and hastening to situate—now—this birth that is fully in the future. The good old days of the first birth of love will be followed, after a lapse of time, by a renewal of that birth. Thus the young poet's thought (and, in its wake, that of the reader) oscillates from the "old new" to the new new, to the new future, without once pausing at the present moment—that is, at the moment we may legitimately consider the only authentically new moment, the *moment in action*.

In this poem on the newness of love, then, love is not directly

47. "Soleil et chair," 44 (33).

considered in its actual immediacy. The new is then not new, and that is why it can be said that the neophyte that Rimbaud was at the time unwittingly bypassed his real subject, the properly Rimbaldian subject, which would have been the experience of love's birth comprehended in its novelty and expressed as such at the moment it occurs.

"Hurrah for the miraculous work and for the marvellous body, for the first time!"[48] Let us note immediately, in these lines from "Matinée d'ivresse"—lines belonging to a much later poem—how different the tone is, and how perfectly the subject is grasped. The same holds true a little later in the same poem, a few lines down: "And now," cries the poet, "let me fervently gather in the superhuman promise made to my created body and soul." It is true, of course, that in this text a promise is mentioned, and any promise refers to a period different from the one in which the promise will be kept. Nevertheless, its fulfillment is presented here the moment it occurs. It is this fulfillment that is new. It occurs within the *now*. Whatever the importance of promises made at other times, only the present fulfillment of those promises captures the poet's attention. The future does not yet exist. The past is past. Without taking the least account of either, I, Rimbaud, give myself to the moment at hand. When I say "hurrah!" in welcoming the "miraculous work" or the "marvelous body," my very cry, my cry of enthusiasm, accurately expresses the exclusive nature of the energy with which I attach myself to what newly occupies the realm of my consciousness. "I am now given over," the poet says, "to a new worry."[49] Each moment he lives, whether in his poetical work or in his life as an adolescent and poet, is a moment of worry, a worry each time renewed. "Sufficient unto the day is the evil thereof," says Ecclesiastes. Sufficient unto the moment is the worry thereof. From moment to moment, and from worry to worry, Rimbaud's existence never manages to constitute a continuous duration. He proceeds in thrusts, with clean severances in between. But it is not the severances that count; it is, rather, the thrusts. They partake of the moment as if it alone existed, with nothing behind it. "Poetry . . . will be in advance."[50] "Departure into new affection and

48. *Illuminations*, "Matinée d'ivresse," 269 (233).
49. Ibid., "Vies," 265 (229).
50. "Lettre à Demeny," 15 May 1871, 348 (309).

sound."[51] It is not an overstatement to say that Rimbaud throws himself upon each moment. His rush to attain it is so hasty that there cannot be the slightest delay in displaying it instantaneously through speech—an essentially exclamatory, often monosyllabic speech, which, like the rooster's crowing of which Rimbaud spoke, is a cry. The "hurrah" welcoming the "miraculous work" is also a cry. All of the poet's writings are punctuated by such cries. One could make a long list of them. Here are just a few examples:

—Ah! what a beautiful morning this New Year's morning!

—Ah! quel beau matin, que ce matin des étrennes![52]

Ah! how sad New Year's Day will be for them!

Oh! que le jour de l'an sera triste pour eux![53]

Oh! oh! what brilliant loves I dreamed of!

Oh! là là! que d'amours splendides j'ai rêvées![54]

But, in truth, I have wept too much!

Mais, vrai, j'ai trop pleuré . . . ![55]

O let my keel burst! O let me go into the sea!

O que ma quille éclate! O que j'aille à la mer![56]

Ah! dust of the willows shaken by a wing!

Ah! la poudre des saules qu'une aile secoue![57]

O Seasons, O castles . . .

O saisons, ô châteaux . . .[58]

Oh! may it live long, each time/The Gallic cock crows.

O vive lui, chaque fois/Que chante le coq gaulois[59]

In truth, this time I wept more than all the children in the world . . .

Vrai, cette fois j'ai pleuré plus que tous les enfants du monde . . .[60]

51. *Illuminations*, "Départ," 266 (247).
52. "Les Etrennes des orphelins," 36 (11).
53. Ibid., 37 (13).   54. "Ma Bohème," 81 (63).
55. "Le Bateau ivre," 131 (119).   56. Ibid.
57. "Mémoire," 178 (125).   58. "O saisons, ô châteaux," 179 (151).
59. Ibid.   60. "Les Déserts de l'amour," 189 (289).

107

Oh! the most violent Paradise of the enraged smile!

O le plus violent Paradis de la grimace enragée![61]

His breathing, his heads, his racings: the terrifying
    swiftness
of form and action when they are perfect.

O ses souffles, ses têtes, ses courses: la terrible célerité
de la perfection des formes et de l'action.[62]

"Rimbaud," writes Benjamin Fondane in *Rimbaud le voyou,*
"wants to *cry out* in poetry itself, to make inspiration and the cry
coincide."[63]

It is exclamation (often a very brief exclamation) that gives
expression not to the mood of the soul but to its movement, the
immediate movement of the feeling the poet experiences. It is the
immediacy of speech that translates, or even anticipates, the immediacy of what is lived inside the poet. Everything in Rimbaldian discourse occurs as if—in order to make it more rapid, to see
it run more quickly toward its outward expression—exclamation
played the role of a signal, instantly warning the reader that, at
that very moment, something new, something sharp as a sword,
is beginning to take place. Just as often, in Rimbaud, the exclamation is immediately introductory: it functions as a threshold instantly crossed in order to partake of the action. The essential
goal of all this in Rimbaud is to *reinforce* the present, to detach it
from what has gone before, to arrange things such that the reader
has the impression that the real action begins at the exact moment
the exclamation is uttered. The same is often true of another
introductory turn of phrase—less ejaculatory, perhaps, but even
more clearly directed toward the present moment, for which it in
some sense serves as an overture. These words are the preposi-
tions here (*voici*) or there (*voilà*). Rimbaud often builds them into a
series. The poem then depends upon a certain number of con-
secutive *heres* and *theres*.

In "Michel et Christine," for example:

    [here] float about . . .
    [here] my spirit flies away . . .
    Behold a thousand wolves . . .

61. *Illuminations,* "Parade," 261 (225).   62. Ibid., "Génie," 308 (255).
63. Benjamin Fondane, *Rimbaud le voyou* (Paris: Denoël, 1933), 79.

Voici nager . . .
Voici que mon esprit vole . . .
Voilà mille loups . . .[64]

Or in "L'Orgie parisienne":

Here are the quays, and the boulevards, here are the
      houses . . .
Here is the red-headed troop of hip wrigglers . . .
See the night of joy . . . , etc.

Voilà les quais, voilà les boulevards, voilà les maisons . . .
Voici le troupeau roux des tordeuses de hanche, . . .
Voici la nuit de joie . . . , etc.[65]

In all these cases, the *here* or *there* seems to be the trigger for an endlessly interrupted motion; a trigger that gives that motion an even better new start. Something similar is to be found in the following couplet:

Oh! there in the middle of the dance of Death
Leaps into the red sky a great mad skeleton.

Oh! voilà qu'au milieu de la danse macabre
Bondit dans le ceil rouge un grand squelette fou.[66]

The leaping referred to here, like the *voilà* which prefigures it, are sudden entries into matter, putting the accent on the rapidity with which another episode occurs. Marcel Raymond's comment can appropriately be quoted here: "Rimbaud's poetry is first a leaping."[67] We shall see this leaping again—no longer exactly in the form of an entry into the present moment but in the surge the present makes to hurl itself beyond, toward the future. In any case, leaping in Rimbaud is not always content to land in the present; it crosses it through and through, and with such speed that it is impossible to speak in this case of a halted present, or of a static present. "Arripui tempus," writes Rimbaud in a Latin poem, one of his earliest works: "I seized the opportunity."[68] This expression must have impressed Rimbaud. That is because it emphasizes the velocity of energy with which the person to whom Rimbaud here refers seizes upon the flight of time granted

---

64. "Michel et Christine," 174 (127).   65. "L'Orgie parisienne," 102 (83).
66. "Bal des pendus," 49 (39).
67. Marcel Raymond, *Vérité et poésie*, (Neuchâtel: Baconnière, 1964), 209.
68. *Vers latins*, "Le Songe de l'écolier," *Oeuvres* (Paris: Pléiade, 1951), 7.

him. It is in this way that Rimbaud, no matter what the period of his life, always acted; seizing with terrible rapidity the opportunity at hand. Here, we are as far removed as possible from the *carpe diem* of the Epicurean poets. They—along with Horace, La Fontaine, Chaulieu, and, especially, Fontenelle—strive to practice an economical utilization of the time immediately allocated to them, in order to savor it morsel by morsel. Hence, the slowing down of the march of time in their works. Rimbaud, on the contrary, lays hold of the moment as if it were his prey. He never attempts to make the present moment last by turning it over slowly in his hands, like a jewel. He is more like a dog rushing to devour his rations. It is a brief joy, born of a moment that itself exists but briefly. A flash of lightning joy. But in this flash there lies the perception of the character of fundamental plenitude that the moment thus possessed can bestow. In the Rimbaldian present, everything seems possessed at once, and not little by little. It is as if the poet—unable, like the Christian divinity, to enjoy an eternal *totum simul,* involving an infinity of simultaneous joys within the continually unchanging present of a perpetual existence—chose to seize whatever he could, but *everything* he could, in each fixed moment of his existence. This is not to deny that, in a passage from "Matinée d'ivresse," Rimbaud described human beings (and, therefore, himself) as unable to "seize [this] eternity on the spot."[69] But that is because the eternity mentioned here is divine, enveloping all of time in a single moment. Such is not the case for *human eternity:* an eternity reduced to the dimensions of man, an eternity untethered to the past, and unextended into the future; an eternity more or less restricted to the present moment.

Rimbaud's way of clutching exclusively at the present seems infinitely removed from the usual steps taken by the human mind to maintain or tighten its bonds with a past or future. Let us first consider the past. In the first of Rimbaud's writings—a piece of Latin verse—one word bursts forth, a word describing the poet himself walking in the countryside. That word is *immemor.*[70] It describes Rimbaud exactly: a being not only devoid of memory but utterly indifferent to the past. Perhaps it is in this light that the great line from "Le Bateau ivre" should be read:

69. *Illuminations,* "Matinée d'ivresse," 269 (233).
70. "Le Songe de l'écolier" (Pléiade), 7.

I was indifferent to all crews.

J'étais insoucieux de tous les équipages.[71]

Indeed, the drunken boat's adventure is connected to no previous history. The wake it leaves is erased. There are no, or few, memories in Rimbaud (except the line from "Le Bateau ivre": "I miss Europe with its ancient parapets!"[72] But has not the drunken boat, at that moment, ceased being intoxicated, and being itinerant as well?). There is, then, no profound nostalgia for the past: "But why regret an eternal sun, if we are committed to the discovery of divine light?"[73] "This hardly makes me miss the world."[74] Such elimination of the past is not restricted to explicit memories or personal regrets. In contrast to most people, Rimbaud refuses to use anything historical as a crutch. "If only I had ancestors at some point in the history of France! No! no antecendent."[75] "What was I in the last century? I recognize myself only today."[76]

Severing all ties with the past, Rimbaud in more than one text breaks his ties with the future as well. No activity is commoner to the human race than the projection of our hopes ahead of us. But if, as we shall see, no thought stands so poised to project itself, to overtake the course of time, to leap madly toward its desires than does Rimbaud's thought—conversely, no thought more brutally denies itself the right to surrender to this weakness called hope: "I was able to expel from my mind all human hope," writes Rimbaud.[77] And elsewhere, referring to that ideal place where there is no future, where there is only an eternal present, he cries, "Here there is no hope—No *orietur*."[78]

To Rimbaud's thinking, there is then no specially reserved place for him in the future, at least in the distant future, the extratemporal or eschatological future. Devoid of hope for an eternal future, and devoid of the memory of an eternal past, Rimbaud is left with no other recourse, it seems, but to situate himself within the extraordinarily narrow walls of the moment at hand.

---

71. "Le Bateau ivre," 128 (115).   72. Ibid., 131 (119).
73. *Une saison en enfer*, "Adieu," 240 (207).
74. Ibid. "Nuit de l'enfer," 222 (185).
75. Ibid., "Mauvais sang," 213 (175).   76. Ibid., 214 (177).
77. Ibid., 211 (173).   78. "L'Eternité," 160 (141).

And yet he makes of this moment, or at least attempts to make of it, a type of trampoline from which he can spring vertically, as it were, into an eternity of his own invention—an eternity that is neither future, nor past, nor infinite, but entirely situated within the present moment.

It is a moment of the present that might be somehow rendered eternal—not by the length of its duration but by the wealth, we might even say the fulmination, of its contents. Rimbaud's ambition is to make of each day, each moment, the equivalent of a lifetime. Thus he gives the lie to the sentence written by his own hand: We cannot "seize its eternity on the spot."[79] To seize on the spot the eternity of which he dreams is precisely what Rimbaud strives for, what he demands of himself. To confer by his own action a particular eternity upon every moment—that, in a nutshell, is the poet's pretension.

It is an inordinate pretension, but one which, far from seeming unattainable to him, seems to him on the contrary in exact proportion to his person. As we have seen, Rimbaud does not consider man to be restricted by his condition as creature. For him, every human creature, and Rimbaud in particular, can, if it so wishes, be capable of creating itself, or of recreating itself, by means of a rigorously personal act. Man is both creator and creature. Therefore, he is at the same time the God who creates him and the being created by that God. If these two contradictory aspects in him do not merge, if a nearly insurmountable distance continues to exist between himself as creator and himself as creature, it is because an infinite separation continues to exist between these two parts of him. If these two sides be joined and merged in the lightning flash of the moment, then man is no longer split into two. The ephemeral but total eternity he enjoys at such moments is precisely this fusion, this intermingling to which his two natures submit:

> It is found again!
> What? Eternity.
> It is the sea mixed
>   With the sun.

---

79. *Illuminations*, "Matinée d'ivresse," 269 (233).

Elle est retrouvée
Quoi?—L'Eternité
C'est la mer mêlée
Au soleil.[80]

10

"IT CAN ALMOST be said without metaphor: Rimbaud is the man exempt from original sin."[81]

This marvelous comment by the great critic Jacques Rivière delineates the precise moral position of Rimbaud and defines as well, when put in the negative, that of Baudelaire.

As I have tried to demonstrate in the entire first half of this book, Baudelaire, in contrast to Rimbaud, was the man who, as long as he lived, never ceased to feel the weight of original sin on his shoulders.

It is a permanent weight for him, a burden that seems impossible for him to shed and that consequently becomes an integral part of his existence. For Baudelaire, original sin is not merely the event that, more than the creation of the world itself, stands at the origin of time. It is also the act which continues indefinitely to exert its influence throughout all of time, and thus links together all moments within time's duration. For Baudelaire, man can never extricate himself—even for an instant—from the constancy of his character created by his perserverence in evil. One can say that for the Baudelairean man, humankind (taken as a whole, with all the individuals it comprises), no matter what the renewal of its actions or thoughts, never manifests its thoughts except as the interminable prolongation of a situation that began with original sin.

It is thus impossible to comprehend the Baudelairean man other than as situated in the chain of sins that he and his race have never ceased committing. Such is true time, and such the very

---

80. *Une saison en enfer*, "Faim," 232 (139).
81. Jacques Rivière, *Rimbaud* (Paris: Emile-Paul ed., 1938?), 44.

fabric of its duration. For Baudelaire, ecstasies, happy moments, paradisiac pauses, are never anything but fleeting truces in the permanent awareness of a culpability both ancestral and personal. Whether he turns to his past or to his future, the author of *Les Fleurs du mal* sees only the persistence of a way of being, composed of errors and shame. No moment of his existence can be truly redeemed. Original sin makes the perenniality of sin felt on all sides.

Could one conceive of a situation more different from Rimbaud's? Rimbaud, as we know, exists only within the moment he lives, and this moment is in no way attached to any preceding event whatever. Rimbaud can address each moment as he does in a text from *Une Saison en enfer:*

> —all my burden is laid aside. Without being dazed, let us evaluate the extent of my innocence.[82]

In this text, it is true, Rimbaud seems to speak the same language as a Christian absolved by his feeling of penitence. As with the Christian, for Rimbaud it is not only a given sin but the whole body of his faults that can be erased by a purifying action, comparable to that accomplished in absolution. But what a difference there is, on the other hand, between the pardoned Christian and the poet delivering himself of his sins! For the former, everything depends upon the power of sacrament and contrition. For the latter, there is a similar return to innocence, but without the mediation of sacrament or remorse, without a repentant return to a life which, surely, throughout its span, could have been considered by him as the life of a sinner. Rimbaud, in fact, never refers to this previous life, except as an "expanse" abruptly relieved of its burden (whatever it may have been), no doubt riddled with error, but error that no longer exists. The innocence of which he speaks is a feeling of irresistible power, but unmotivated and so sudden in its intervention that it remains almost inexplicable. Once again, an entirely new existence unfolds.

Moreover, it is an existence without duration. It is rigorously confined to the present minute. Rimbaud writes: "This moment of awakening gave me the vision of purity.[83]

82. *Une saison en enfer,* "Mauvais sang," 218 (181).
83. Ibid., "L'Impossible," 237 (205).

Indeed, as we have seen from the first pages of this essay, the "moment of awakening" is always the most important moment for Rimbaud; even more, as Nerval would say, the "unique moment," since it is the one in which time begins anew. It is a virginal time; a time without sin or stain. "I have not committed evil," Rimbaud says.[84] That is because, for him, the only times that exist or subsist are virginal. The rest are worthless or canceled out. They leave no trace in the mind, no regrets in the emotions. Innocence retrieved—we might say *endlessly awakened*—has the effect of nullifying all past errors—sometimes throwing those errors back onto other people. "My innocence has been abused," writes Rimbaud.[85]

Except in the end, or in a few exceptional circumstances such as, perhaps, that recapitulation of his life called *Une saison en enfer*, we really never see Rimbaud admit to his faults or even recognize their persistent nature. If there is blame, it is most often leveled at others.

It is true that Rimbaud also wrote: "What soul is without flaws?"[86] But we should not see in this a way of claiming that everyone, including him, falls into sin. In fact, Rimbaud believes—quite sincerely—that if there is a soul without flaw, it is his own. He does not believe it because he is blind to himself, or self-satisfied, but because that has been his experience: the experience of an innocence perpetually rediscovered, which can never be denied, which can only be, from time to time, temporarily suspended.

All consciousness of his own innocence, as Rimbaud experiences it, must necessarily be in the present. Each time it occurs, it is a recovery of self comparable to Adam's frame of mind at the time of Eden: "It is true: I was thinking of Eden!"[87] Rimbaud admits one day. One should not see in this, as one does in Baudelaire's work, the confession of nostalgic feelings. If Rimbaud occasionally thinks of Eden, it is because the moments that inspire that thought are themselves Edenic. Within each of them, Rimbaud becomes aware of his innocence. In contrast to Baudelaire, who, even when he dreams of an earthly paradise, seems

---

84. Ibid., "Mauvais sang," 217 (181).
85. "Brouillon d'*Une saison en enfer*," 353.
86. *Une saison en enfer*, 234 (201).   87. Ibid., "L'Impossible," 236 (203).

never to forget that his ancestors' transgressions as well as his own keep him eternally separated from it, for Rimbaud to dream of Eden is to dream of a paradise that can always begin anew, as if the Fall had never occurred. The time of Eden is not, for our poet, a historical time. It is less a *time* than the reiteration of kind of present moment.

11

A TIME OF INNOCENCE and of purity; a time of perfection; a time indefinitely renewable. A time enjoyed by the magi and, even more, by the angels. "I who called myself magus or angel," writes Rimbaud, adding in a manner nevertheless a bit surprising, "exempt from all morality."[88]

The fact is that, for Rimbaud, angelic purity does not only have a positive aspect. It also has a negative aspect; even a violently negative one. For Rimbaud, the angel or the magus has the privilege of situating himself outside of, or beyond, all morals. He is a Nietzschean angel.

He is an angel blessed with a kind of active purity, yet a terribly aggressive angel (one thinks of Louis Antoine Saint-Just). A furious angel, absorbed in his task of overthrowing, shattering, collapsing all institutions, all orders, all social and individual existence. In this phase of Rimbaldian poetry, nothing positive is to be sought, no moderation, no attenuation of wrath, not even the simplest soothing of temper. We are submitted to a breathless, precipitant rhythm, like a string of curses, an almost uninterrupted series of maledictions of every sort conceivable. It is a continuous assault; not only an assault of sarcasm and blasphemy but one bolstered by words as violent as instruments of war; a movement of insurrection of unbelievable brutality, whose goal is to overthrow everything standing erect. It is the work of a revolutionary and, of course, of an anarchist. It is a project that deliberately sets out to destroy the social order. But there is more—that is, even worse (or better). Here destruction goes infi-

88. Ibid., "Adieu," 240 (209).

nitely beyond the walls of institutions; it aims at another order, one no less solidly rooted—at least in appearance—than the social order. It seeks to attack the moral order itself, there where it seems on the contrary most unassailable and invulnerable. No doubt, within the lucid delirium transporting him, Rimbaud appears as himself carried away, as giving in to the popular momentum, as playing his part in a united offensive front. But this should not be taken to be a simple walking-on part. He personally raises the flag of revolt, and—in his expressions and feelings, if not in his actions, in his audacity, intransigence, in the extraordinarily menacing tone of his words—he is among those who distinguish themselves in the front lines, in the heat of battle. An example of this is to be found in an untitled poem, which begins with the words, "What does it matter for us, my heart . . .":

> What does it matter for us, my heart, the sheets of blood
> And coals, and a thousand murders, and the long cries
> Of rage, sobs from every hell upsetting
> Every order; and the north wind still over the debris;
> And all vengeance? Nothing! But yes, still,
> We want it! Industrialists, princes, senates:
> Perish! Power, justice, history: down with you!
> That is our due. Blood! blood! golden flame!
> All to war, to vengeance and to terror,
> My spirit!

> *Qu'est-ce pour nous, mon cœur, que les nappes de sang*
> *Et de braise, et mille meurtres, et les longs cris*
> *De rage, sanglots de tout enfer renversant*
> *Tout ordre; et l'Aquilon encor sur les débris;*
> *Et toute vengeance? Rien.—Mais si, toute encor,*
> *Nous la voulons! Industriels, princes, sénats,*
> *Périssez! puissance, justice, histoire, à bas!*
> *Ça nous est dû. Le sang! le sang! la flamme d'or!*
> *Tout à la guerre, à la vengeance, à la terreur,*
> *Mon esprit!*[89]

In what other poet writing of the collapsed Second Empire could we find such an outburst of destructive words? No doubt, this is armchair violence. Rimbaud, as we know, did not participate in the Commune, not, at least, personally or actively. In the

---

89. "Qu'est-ce pour nous, mon cœur . . ." 171 (125, 127).

extreme youth that limits his actions, yet without in the least restraining the expression of his hatred, Rimbaud is a person who, far from letting himself be merged with the mob, naturally goes to the forefront—not to add to the crowd but to leave all the others behind by the immeasurable intensity of his passion. Every word in this poem acts as a staggering blow. Every shaft aims for only one thing: to hit the person or object on which it is trained as hard as possible. Rimbaud seeks above all to cause a general collapse of things. But this collapse is in itself so dramatic only because there is a will to hasten it, pressing upon it without respite, unceasingly insisting upon completion. This will manifests itself as being fundamentally destructive; but in itself it does not differ from the essentially creative activity of which we have already spoken at length.

In short, for Rimbaud the act of destruction is not fundamentally different from the act of creation. Or, rather, destruction for him is so obvious a phenomenon, occupying so visible a space, that it does not appear as pure and simple obliteration but as the most practical means of realizing the transmutation of the real. If destruction is not the immediate creator, at least it creates the indispensable shock that clears the way for genuine creation. We can find an example of this in the poet's work by examining the role played in it by the phenomenon of denudation. By stripping (most often brutally) a person or thing of its normal appearance, the poet makes the real, naked presence emerge before our eyes. Such is the case in the poem entitled "Le Châtiment de Tartufe":

> One day as he walked along, "Let us pray,"—a wicked
> fellow
> Seized him roughly by his blessed ear
> And hurled frightful words at him as he tore off
> The chaste black robe about his moist skin.

> *Un jour qu'il s'en allait, "Oremus,"—un Méchant*
> *Le prit rudement par son oreille benoîte*
> *Et lui jeta des mots affreux, en arrachant*
> *Sa chaste robe noire autour de sa peau moite!*[90]

90. "Le Châtiment de Tartufe," 50 (39).

In the poem "Le Forgeron," already cited, we witness with the insurgents the destruction of the Bastille. And from this destruction, there immediately emerges a highly positive image:

—Citizen! citizen! it was the dark past
Crumbling, giving its death-rattle, when we took the
    tower!
Something like love was in our hearts.

Citoyen! citoyen! c'était le passé sombre
Qui croulait, qui râlait, quand nous prîmes la tour!
Nous avions quelque chose au cœur comme l'amour.[91]

It is clear that the process of Rimbaldian creation entails not only the collapse of the past but the liberation of the present as well. Or, more precisely: it is a creation that allows for the emergence, in the place left open by the disappearance of the past, of a time that is no longer an abolished past but asserts itself as a new, free, and present time. Thus violence, cruelty, even murder itself can be the means by which a new time is uncovered; a time that can be a sudden and terribly positive joy: "Can man reach esctasy in destruction and be rejuvenated by cruelty?" asks the poet.[92] The answer, clearly, is affirmative. The practice of evil can, in itself, be condemned. But its violence or excesses can create a type of hiatus in the course of time's continuity. For when that continuity is suddenly interrupted, a new time appears and fills the gap. What Rimbaud calls "the age of murderers"[93] may be precisely this exchange of times.

Murderers of others, but also of ourselves. Suicide, which is the total destruction of a previous ego, makes possible the birth of a new ego. Rimbaud's life is then structured as a series of attempts on the life of more or less everyone but, in particular and above all, on his own life. The property of destruction is to produce a hole, a stoppage, and, at the moment of that stoppage, a shock, a resumption of life. If Rimbaud seeks to make a monster of his soul, it is because the monstrous denaturating of his being is a destruction offering him the possibility of liberation.

---

91. "Le Forgeron," 53 (21).   92. *Illuminations*, "Conte," 259 (225).
93. Ibid., "Matinée d'ivresse," 269 (233).

12

WHETHER MANIFEST IN THE realm of politics or in that of social, religious, familial, or even individual customs, the liberation Rimbaud so passionately seeks is most likely to choose, as we have just seen, the path of extreme violence.

"But we are free,"[94] said the blacksmith impudently and aggressively in the poem by Rimbaud on which I have already commented.

Of course, the words Rimbaud puts into the mouth of the old republican of 1789 express the sentiments of the adolescent poet during the time of the Commune. The same holds true for an entire series of rather declamatory, but clearly sincere, poems by the same author. Consider for example the following selection— two quatrains:

> Dead of '92 and '93,
> Who, pale from the hard kiss of freedom,
> Calm, broke, under your clogs, the yoke which weighs
> On the soul and the brow of all humanity;
>
> Men exalted and noble in the storm,
> You whose hearts leapt with love under your rags,
> O soldiers whom Death, lofty Mistress, has sown
> In all the old furrows, in order to regenerate them . . .
>
> *Morts de Quatre-vingt-douze et de Quatre-vingt-treize,*
> *Qui, pâles du baiser fort de la liberté,*
> *Calmes, sous vos sabots, brisiez le joug qui pèse*
> *Sur l'âme et sur le front de toute humanité;*
>
> *Hommes extasiés et grands dans la tourmente,*
> *Vous dont les cœurs sautaient d'amour sous les haillons,*
> *O soldats que la Mort a semés, noble Amante,*
> *Pour les regénérer, dans tous les vieux sillons . . .*[95]

It is not difficult, in these lines, to point once again to what has just been demonstrated: the appetite for violence which Rimbaud never fails to reveal at every opportunity. But there is something more, or different: the metamorphosis of the destroyer by the act

94. "Le Forgeron," 56 (25).
95. "Morts de Quatre-vingt-douze . . ." 63 (53).

of destruction. The experience of the freedom so ardently desired and so aggressively acquired is not, then, a simple negative experience for the young poet. Whoever liberates himself through action, through zeal, and through death is not a pure breaker of yokes. He is in Rimbaud's own words an exalted man. No doubt the type of heroic euphoria that seized the soldiers of the Year II mentioned here, belong to a certain aspect of poetry which is both epic and popular, to which Rimbaud was sympathetic. They are the "chromo" side of a military lithograph. But these lines, with their obvious naiveté (which plays a considerable role in the mentality of the adolescent that Rimbaud was at the time) also translate the state of mind of one to whom liberty—no matter how it is won—is always a creative emancipation. Liberty is the magical transformation of a state of hostility and negative violence, into its opposite, a state of positive freedom, achieved through the very violence with which it manifests itself. It is, to use Rimbaud's marvelous expression from one of his letters, a "free freedom."[96]

Such is the state of mind represented more or less symbolically by Rimbaud in one of his most famous poems, "Le Bateau ivre." For this poem, read at its most obvious level, is nothing other than a work whose subject is the emancipation of man through his own action. It is the story of a man who has broken his shackles and who, henceforth without chains, *having created by a purposeful act* the conditions of his freedom, wanders at will in the marine expanses he explores:

> Free, smoking, topped with violet fog,
> I who pierced the reddening sky like a wall . . .

> *Libre, fumant, monté de brumes violettes,*
> *Moi qui trouais le ciel rougeoyant comme un mur . . .*[97]

It becomes more than evident that, between the proclamation the boat makes of its freedom and the opening it has pierced in the wall of space, there is a relationship of the greatest significance. If the boat is able to be in possession of itself in its newly acquired freedom, if it becomes conscious—with the exaltation we already know of—of the free path it follows (or rather has

96. "Lettre à Izambard," 2 November, 1870, *Œuvres* (Pléiade), 248 (301).
97. "Le Bateau ivre," 130 (119).

chosen to follow) on the sea, it is because it has effected, and will continue to effect, an opening in the wall of existence. The boat has delivered itself of the ties that bound it, of the pilot who could determine its position in a place not of its choosing. The boat has—at least, partially—achieved its own deliverance. And it is a deliverance that it continues to enjoy as it pursues its journey. Every incident, every new encounter, every danger is an occasion for it to reinvent the act by which it pierced that first opening. All of the rest of the episodes in "Le Bateau ivre" depend upon a point of departure that is the control over its own destiny achieved by that being who is the boat's soul. In a way, no doubt, this being's odyssey depends upon an initial event in which it does not seem to have been in a position to take an active part: the massacre of the haulers by the Redskins—that is, an enemy from the outside. But Rimbaud, on the other hand, takes care to suggest us that the situation created by this killing is not only accepted, but acknowledged, by the boat itself. Its drifting, its descent down the rivers, its entry into the ocean are not passively submitted to. On the contrary, everything occurs as if the boat were seizing the opportunity to escape the control to which it had been previously subjugated. No more rudder, no more grappling iron! The drunken boat takes charge of its own freedom and, consequently, itself chooses the path that this acquired freedom allows it to pursue. Everything in the poem expresses a simultaneous mixture of risk and ardor: the departure, the courses followed, the numerous incidents along the way. But everything is also inspired by a freedom of the greatest elation. "Le Bateau ivre" is the poem of freedom in action, endlessly initiating new manifestations of freedom, in repeated surges.

The violence—at least, the exaltation—and the ardor are then the first features emphasized by Rimbaud when he wants to describe the individual who has conquered his freedom. The mood of the very young man who wrote this poem must have been, if not violent, at least spasmodically unbridled, proceeding by sudden explosions in the wake of *bonaces*—that is, periods of relaxation or apparent lulls. But in order to free himself of the shackles he could barely tolerate, there were other means besides fits of rage. There was, for example, cold contempt, silent disdain for those men or women who held him in loathesome captivity:

"I was right in all my scorn," he writes, "since I am escaping."[98] Nevertheless, disdain is merely a last resort, even a defeat, since it implies abstention from, or renunciation of, action. It is better to act at the interior, to act mentally—that is, to escape through dreaming, since the dream is a form of internal action. It is no doubt in this sense that a poem like "Ophélie," portraying the drowning of a young girl, is to be interpreted. While still alive, she had heard the winds whisper to her of freedom; finally, to attain this freedom, she had chosen death:

> Heaven! Love! Freedom! What a dream, oh poor mad girl!
> You melted to him as snow to a fire.
>
> *Ciel! Amour! Liberté! Quel rêve, ô pauvre folle!*
> *Tu te fondais à lui comme une neige au feu.*[99]

This dream of freedom can be seen again in another of Rimbaud's poems, "Les Poètes de sept ans":

> At seven, he wrote novels about the life
> In the great desert, where exiled Freedom shines,
> Forests, suns, riverbanks, plains!
>
> *A sept ans, il faisait des romans sur la vie*
> *Du grand désert, où luit la Liberté ravie,*
> *Forêts, soleils, rives, savanes.*[100]

The great open spaces of James Fenimore Cooper's plains have the same role in Rimbaud's imagination as does Shakespearean death. In both cases, the poet, as he says in *Une saison en enfer*, seeks only one thing: "to escape from reality."[101] Death and myth are, precisely, unreal, accommodating themselves better to the infinite desire for freedom than to the daily duties of family life. Death and myth are unlimited, almost formless, and, therefore, provide more space. Yet there is another kind of free space: the sky itself. It is characteristic of Rimbaud's work that the sky never plays the role, as it does in Baudelaire, of an expanse in which he might dream of losing himself. Or, at least, if he does conceive of it at all in this manner, it is as a space delivered of the

---

98. *Une saison en enfer,* "L'Impossible," 235 (203).   99. "Ophélie," 47 (37).
100. "Les Poètes de sept ans," 96 (77).
101. *Une saison en enfer,* "Délires," 225 (189).

divinities that encumber it. In a well-known passage in "Soleil et chair," the poet imagines man as "weary of smashing idols" but ready to be resurrected," free of all his gods,"[102] into a cloudless sky in which he will at last move freely. Once again, nothing could contrast more sharply with Baudelaire's point of view. For the latter, no escape is possible; for how can one be extricated from the situation in which mankind is placed as the direct result of original sin? Moreover, despite many efforts to reach a free, open space, the Baudelairean man never escapes. He is condemned to live in a closed space. The sky is usually beyond his reach. Conversely, Rimbaud never gives up his struggle for open space. He, like the drunken boat, is "an escape expert."

He does, further, and above all, make passionate use of open space. No matter what its properties may be—properties of which I shall speak at greater length below—space is above all for Rimbaud that dimension of reality which, unencumbered as far as the eye can see, without obstacles, open to anyone who would venture in it, permits the mind to enter it anywhere and in any way it chooses. One is reminded of a line from "Bateau ivre":

> The Rivers let me go where I wanted.
>
> *Les fleuves m'ont laissé descendre où je voulais.*[103]

Space is like rivers (and, even more, like the ocean). One can travel within it unimpeded; and, within its expanses, one can make an infinity of forms emerge to people it. Thus the rivers and seas that the boat plows reveal monsters haunting their chasms—even more frequently monsters born of, or at least extracted from, the abyss by the boat itself on its journey. For the most part, the drunken boat appears incontestably the creator of what it encounters or, more precisely, of what it instigates. It is as if the privilege granted it to sail in an element itself devoid of all landmarks gives the boat, as it moves forward within that element, the capacity to call into existence all sorts of shapes and forms, even the most bizarre, at the will of an infinitely capricious thought; a thought that feels singularly at ease to invent what it pleases. And, in the same measure as it invents what it pleases, it invents itself. "Le Bateau ivre" is like many figures invented in the *Illuminations.* It is the manifestation of a creative power

102. "Soleil et chair," 42 (29).   103. "Le Bateau ivre," 128 (115).

which, without previous determination from the outside, totally "at liberty," as we say, draws from its most intimate resources the faculty to appear in full daylight in any given form. The creative power surrounds itself at will with its creations, and even merges with them.

13

WE SHOULD NOW RECALL that in "Le Bateau ivre," as in some of Hugo's poems, the vision that is revealed most often opens out onto the future. Here we come upon a Rimbaldian point of view profoundly different from the one we considered in discussing *waking*. The consciousness of a being who awakens to rediscover the world is characterized by a contact with *what is*. With the disappearance of night and sleep, before the awakened sleeper manifests any particular interest in what might have occurred he is exclusively concerned with what offers itself directly to his gaze or thought. He has not yet had the time to think or see beyond this. The instantaneous consciousness of self, the no less instantaneous discovery of the world with which he is directly confronted, absorb all his attention. He limits himself to embracing, with all his strength, the moment he is living.

But quite often in Rimbaud—and with increasing frequency as he progresses in his poetic enterprise—a distinctly different way of experiencing time can be discerned. To awaken, to open one's eyes, to be in contact with the world—all this is no longer necessarily a sudden vision of what is for him; it is also quite frequently a presentiment of what will be. Or, more precisely, it is the moment in which existence is grasped, no longer in its pure present but in the movement by which it becomes *other*. Or, to give a third definition of this change that is perceived the moment Rimbaud is becoming aware of himself, what he is trying to catch unawares (and to express) here is less the state than the passage, the process (often difficult to perceive) by which, under the poet's own impulse, what is real changes in substance or in appearance and gives way to the dreamed, to desire, to the invented. Rimbaud is not only the poet of the present moment. He is, and almost by the same token, the poet of a present that changes into the future. Hence the title Jean-Pierre Richard gives to his essay on Rimbaud: "Rimbaud, or the Poetry of Becoming."[104]

In Rimbaud's earliest writings one can already see aspects of this point of view, although they are rather clumsily expressed. Indeed, it would be difficult to avoid seeing in these texts the already considerable weight given to the theme of the future, especially the immediate future. As I have already noted, the poem "Sensation" is entirely constructed with verbs of the future: "I will go . . . I will feel . . . I will not speak . . . I will have no thoughts . . . infinite love will mount in my soul," etc. In longer poems of the same period, the entire narration is constructed in two tenses: one past, the other future. Thought is transported between one and the other. In all of these examples the dominant feeling is that of an imminent future, one called to existence, which we can sense will not be long in taking the place of a present already out of date.

The same holds true for another series of poems ("Le Réparties de Nina," "Rêve pour l'hiver," etc.) in which the poet, situating himself in the moment at hand, tries to depict a future that his imagination constructs in advance. The future tense he employs is less a real future than a hypothetical one, hastily evoked in the present moment by the impatient thought of the one who dreams it. But how different these mental games are from the grandiose vision of the future that unfolds before our eyes in the most admirable line from "Le Bateau ivre":

> Million golden birds, O future vigor!
>
> *Million d'oiseaux d'or, ô future vigueur!*

Yet there is a similarity between the facile lines cited earlier and, on the other hand, the great Rimbaldian line cited here. In both cases, there is a perception of the link the mind establishes between the present time and a subsequent one, which overtakes the first considerably in achieving that link.

One can clearly see this juncture of two times between which, because they do not touch each other, thought progresses with a kind of leap, jumping from one to the other, in the following passages from *Illuminations*:

104. Jean-Pierre Richard, *Poésie et profondeur*, 187.

Along the countryside, streaked with bands of rare music, I created phantoms of a future night parade.[105]

. . . You will begin this work. All the possibilities of harmony and architecture will rise up around your seat. Perfect and unpredictable beings will offer themselves for your experiments. . . . Your memory and your senses will only serve to feed your creative urge.[106]

These two texts allow us to understand that, for Rimbaud, the passage from the present to the future—from decision to action, from the immediate to that which is becoming—can only occur in the form of an inventive, voluntary, and rapid intervention on the part of the subject, who works out his initial resolution by making it pass from its original stage of bursting forth to that of existence within time. This second time is that of the future.

This in no way implies that the original moment in Rimbaldian poetry is somehow incomplete. On the contrary, we have seen that, for the poet of the *Illuminations*, nothing is more important, more decisive, and even more complete in its ultracondensed form than the initial experience which, emerging from the sleep of night, rings the waking bell of existence. That is why this experience, severing itself irremediably from the antecedent vacuity, asserts itself from the outset as a new time; self-sufficient, containing a thousand treasures within its narrow confines. One can return endlessly, in Rimbaud, to an immediate abundance in which everything is implicated. But most often in the poet's works, another stage follows the initial burst of thought—a stage in which the first movement is propagated as it progresses. It is then that thought becomes genuinely creative by expanding its field of action, by ranging across a wider space, and above all by obeying, throughout its course, the "creative impulse" of which the poet speaks. It would indeed be a serious error to assume that, in being propelled under the control of this impulse, the experience at hand, projected as it is in the flow of time, is deprived—even slightly—of the surge that has propelled it. On the contrary, it is a trait fundamental to the life of feelings and ideas in the work of Rimbaud that these impulses never weaken and never lose any of the vigor that was theirs when they were first

105. *Illuminations*, "Vagabonds," 278 (233).   106. Ibid., "Jeunesse," 298 (221).

put into action. For him, from the first moment of thought, images and speech leap into motion. And they leap into the second motion, too, which carries all of their moving parts toward the future.

Indeed, few words return to Rimbaud's vocabulary with such frequency as do: "impetus" (*élan*), "soaring" (*essor*), "flight" (*envol*), "leap" (*bond*), "leaping" (*bondissement*). Some can already be found in a fairly early, particularly juvenile poem, which I have cited before. "Le Bal des pendus."

> Oh! there in the middle of the dance of Death
> Leaps into the red sky a great mad skeleton
> Carried off by his impetus, like a horse rearing.
>
> *Oh! violà qu'au milieu de la danse macabre*
> *Bondit dans le ciel rouge un grand squelette fou*
> *Emporté par l'élan, comme un cheval se cabre.*[107]

Let us not pause over the obviously extravagent character of these ultraromantic images. Rimbaud will do better as time goes on. But let us note the fact that, beginning with this very early poem, there appears a feature that will frequently return in later writings: I am referring to the fact that this leaping consists not only in the suddenness of the initial activity that appears on the stage but also in the immediate, almost redoubled, prolongation of this activity beyond the moment of its first manifestation. Here the impetus, or leap, is not instantaneous. More precisely, it comprises two stages: the first traces the kind of break produced, within a relatively stable situation, by an event exclusively concerned with the present moment; the second, following instantly upon the first, consists in the extension of this event beyond the moment in which it comes upon us. It is as if the event in question, of itself or through the effect of a propulsion inherent to its nature all at once, the moment after it was born, could not cease to exist, and were about to metamorphose itself into a phenomenon of duration. In Rimbaud this is quite frequently the case. The first leaping, the soaring, the flight becomes the point of departure for what will instantly follow. Once there is a given interruption of time—often a brutal interruption—something like a new beginning of time occurs, proceeding by fits and starts. The

107. "Bal des pendus," 49 (39).

Rimbaldian man, regaining his balance, takes off with renewed vigor. Many texts, especially those in *Illuminations*, are constructed in this way. It is not difficult to give a catalog—and an incomplete one at that—of these:

> Seen enough . . . Had enough . . . Known enough . . . Departure into new affection and sound.[108]

> A tap with your finger on the drum releases all sounds and begins the new harmony.[109]

> One step of yours, and the new men rise up and march.[110]

> For sale . . . Wealth rising up at each step! . . . wild and infinite leap to invisible splendor.[111]

> Let him die as he leaps through unheard of and unnamable things.[112]

> This is the real march. Forward, men![113]

It is true that all of these texts differ in content, orientation, and tone. But they have in common the presentation of the poet's thought as pursuing a march, which begins with a shock and which, very rapidly, through the satisfaction it gives to the mind, risks making the marcher lose the reasons for which he began marching. Then a great change occurs in him. His march becomes an excursion, whose charm consists almost exclusively in the displacement it provides from the usual surroundings. We know how much the "man of the winged shoes" loved to walk. Jacques Plessen has written an excellent book on this subject, entitled *L'expérience de la marche et du mouvement dans l'œuvre de Rimbaud*. The following sentence is to be found in this work; a sentence that merits citation because it formulates with precision what the experience of walking meant to our poet: "In an excercise such as walking, everything occurs as if man . . . behaved like an absolute freedom, majestically laying the foundations of its ties to a world eternally being born."[114]

---

108. *Illuminations,* "Départ," 266 (247).   109. Ibid., "A une raison," 268 (247).
110. Ibid.   111. *Illuminations,* "Solde," 293 (255).
112. "Lettre à Demeny," 15 May 1871, 346 (307).
113. *Illuminations,* "Démocratie," 307 (223).
114. Jacques Plessen, *Promenade et poésie, l'expérience de la marche et du mouvement dans l'œuvre de Rimbaud* (La Haye: Mouton, 1967), 30.

This world born eternally, which at every step begins to live anew, bears but a distant relation to the real places on which the walker's shoes trample. Let us not attempt, therefore, to situate it somewhere on the outside. Let us see it primarily as a fiction created by the walker, as the reflection of images which he himself foments and projects upon the countryside he is crossing. Indeed, we have seen that Rimbaud is above all one who "awakes" from moment to moment; that is, who begins to live anew. Walking is a muscular effort whose rhythm harmonizes with this continually renewed "waking." Each step appears as a leap of the body, accompanying and, to a certain extent, determining the leap of the mind. It is a repeated "Forward, march!" lasting in its repetition. It is of little importance, then, where or whither one walks. It is better if these places remain vague, and vague as well the point at which the walker began his walk. He can thus progress in a space that is tied to nothing behind or in front of him. It is like a mental expanse that gradually unfolds around him; like a kind of huge screen onto which his thought may project what it likes. In walking, then, the walker creates his own space. He only treads on a virgin space, and on the paths of a nameless country. His walk leaves him without ties, without a home, without a family, without a native land—that is, exempt from all previous bonds to whatever place he has left. Rimbaud always had a passion for this experience of open space. When he describes himself, he even chooses to emphasize this character, free of hearth and country, whom he prides himself in being. As early as "Les Etrennes des orphelins" the entire story revolves around "a nest without feathers," an "empty room," and parents who are dead or absent.[115] In "Les Déserts de l'amour" he refers to himself as "a young, a very young man, whose life evolved in no particular place; without a mother, without a country."[116] And elsewhere he writes, "I shall never have enough of seeing myself in that past. But always alone. Without a family."[117] If, contrary to his usual practice, he briefly consents to seeing himself "in that past" in the latter text, it is a past denuded of all that might have furnished it, the past of someone who, at

115. "Les Etrennes des orphelins," 35 (11).
116. "Les Déserts de l'amour," 187 (287).
117. *Une saison en enfer*, "Mauvais sang," 214 (177).

every stage of his life, wishes to be alone. It is a solitude that is assumed so that nothing will be left behind: no regrets, no memory of a beloved, no home to which one might wish to return, to settle in. Nothing in the walker's consciousness survives, save the stretch of road he is following. He walks as if in a dream, or even in a void. If he is leaving, "his fists in his torn pockets,"[118] it is because his pockets are empty; and since the coat he is wearing is designed to contain nothing, the only thing that counts for him is to continue walking and to continue to feel the joy of confronting space. For the walker, there is on the one hand himself, becoming conscious of himself, feeling himself going forth, no matter what the direction; on the other hand, there is also the awareness of being in the presence of a space which, undetermined by any intention to arrive at a particular place, opens out onto all directions with indifference and, with the same indifference, makes them all equal.

Hence the walker's strange exultation in feeling himself to be at a perpetual crossroad, that is, in contact not with a fixed point in space but with space itself, in the multiplicity of directions it comprises. Rimbaud's world is then the opposite of a closed world. It is a world fundamentally open, a type of denuded expanse whose directions all seem of equal value and interchangeable. The expression that best characterizes it is "anywhere" [n'importe où] or "everywhere" [partout],[119] so long as we understand that the "everywhere" here does not represent the integral totality of space. Pursuing his walk without stopping to rest, and therefore always having the same experience, the walker—no matter where he may be—always finds himself in essentially the same situation and in the same place. His singular ubiquity, far from implying a complete possession of space, would rather reveal the capacity to treat it as an anonymous highway along which, as we have seen, the pedestrian as he passes can raise at will any imaginary figure he desires. Everything is presented as if the association between the walker and the country through which he passes consisted for the former in putting into the latter, as into an empty frame, all sorts of dreamed landscapes,

---

118. "Ma Bohème," 81 (63).
119. *Illuminations*, "A une raison," 268 (247); *Une saison en enfer*, "Mauvais sang," 216 (179).

which can be discerned without difficulty against the white backdrop of space.

Against a space that remains unchanged, perpetually empty, located anywhere, a chain of images arises, which could be any images whatever. No individual can be less constrained to remaining faithful to the reality he perceives than this strange walker who bypasses what he sees without deigning to acknowledge it. Rimbaud the walker is utterly uninterested in the real. His passion is inspired only by the possible—or, rather, by things that are possible. Moreover, his experience with external space always results in its replacement by a strictly interior space; a space peopled with interchangeable forms that the walker draws out of his thought by turns as he walks along. In short, instead of following a predetermined itinerary, he takes advantage here of the physical movement of walking to project upon the screen of his mind, one after the other, at will, what he calls "every possible landscape."[120]

"The walker," writes Yves Bonnefoy in referring to Rimbaud, "takes a short cut through the opacity of the real . . . Everything proves to be possible, and the language of poetry is reborn in this possible, merged with it."[121]

14

LET US REMEMBER the famous passage in a letter Rimbaud writes to his friend Delahaye, in which he describes himself at three o'clock in the morning, at dawn, listening to the simultaneous awakening of the birds:

> Last month, my room, on rue Monsieur-le-Prince, looked out on a garden of the lycée Saint-Louis. There were huge trees under my narrow window. At three in the morning, the candle goes pale: all the birds cry at once in the trees: it is over.[122]

120. *Une saison en enfer*, "Alchimie du verbe," 228 (193).
121. Yves Bonnefoy, *Rimbaud par lui-même* (Paris: Seuil, 1961), 33.
122. "Lettre à Delahaye," June 1872, 351 (317).

Jean-Pierre Richard has commented on this text compellingly: "In this temporal hole, this perceptible hiatus called dawn," he writes, "we have the sudden explosion of power and of thought; a sudden spurt of existence."[123] These last two expressions formulate, in admirably well-chosen terms, the features, almost diametrically opposite that the Rimbaldian experience manifests. On the one hand we find here what I myself attempted to describe at the beginning of this study: the spurting, explosive character offered the poet by that which is so often the point of departure for all of his thoughts—the moment of awakening. It is a first moment, fundamental, from which the world and the ego seem once again to come into existence. There can be no doubt that, from this perspective, for Rimbaud (or, as in this case, for the Rimbaldian world), waking forms an experience that is essentially *one*, beyond analysis, individual, an event without precedent and without duration, in which everything in the synthesis it presents is absolutely in the present. The world and the ego explode *at once*. But, on the other hand, this experience is similar to a *spurt*, to use Richard's expression. That is, it is like a composite movement that marks the transition from a spurting to a splash. A more precise image than this is not to be found. The phenomenon of waking, as described by Rimbaud, begins with a spurt, which is then changed into an infinite number of splashes. In short, what appears here in Rimbaud's text and, in particular, in the sentence "all the birds cry at once" is the image of a plurality emerging in unity or, more accurately, *springing from this initial unity*. It is an extremely frequent phenomenon in Rimbaud, one of which there are many examples.

Here is one, among others, which describes what is essentially the same hour of the day:

> In the right-hand corner of the park the summer dawn stirs up leaves and mists and noises, and the mounds on the left-hand side hold in their purple shade the countless swift ruts of the wet road. Fairy procession.[124]

Everything begins with that unique phenomenon: waking. Everything is then revealed as having a thousand details, which both excite and divide attention.

123. Jean-Pierre Richard, *Poésie et profondeur*, 189.
124. *Illuminations*, "Ornières," 275 (239).

This phenomenon is to be found so often that I am prompted to give a few more examples:

> In the cities the mud seemed to me suddenly red and black, like a mirror when the lamp moves about in the next room, like a treasure in the forest! Good luck, I cried, and I saw a sea of flames and smoke in the red sky; and on the left and on the right, every kind of richness flaming like a billion thunderbolts.[125]

> A flight of red pigeons thunders around my thoughts.[126]

> Can I describe the vision? The air of hell does not permit hymns. They were millions of charming creatures.[127]

> A Genie appeared, of unspeakable, unmentionable beauty. His face and his bearing gave promise of a rich complex love, of an indescribable, unbearable happiness.[128]

It is clear how this phenomenon evolves. Attention is first drawn to a unity that is synthetic in nature; then the unity fragments and makes room for the multiplicity of constituent elements. Everything—not only outside, in the spectacles offered by the external world, but also inside, in the poet's imagination—tends to lose its original simplicity and to proliferate, at times abnormally. It is as if, for the poet, this multiplication—far from being the result of external causes—were the result of the direct, all-powerful activity of creative force; such that the poet, in the course of creating, becomes, in his own words, "a multiplier of progress."[129] As the prodigious adolescent that was Rimbaud progresses with bewildering speed toward maturity, we see in him the gradual growth of this power, which consists in substituting a variety of increasingly luxuriant and diversified forms for the relatively somber reality of sensory experience. "I became a fabulous opera . . . To each being it seemed to me that several other lives were due."[130] Starting with any given experience,

125. *Une saison en enfer,* "Mauvais sang," 216 (179).
126. *Illuminations,* "Vies," 264 (229).
127. *Une saison en enfer,* "Nuit de l'enfer," 220 (183).
128. *Illuminations,* "Conte," 259 (225).
129. "Lettre à Demeny," 15 May 1871, 347 (309).
130. *Une saison en enfer,* "Faim," 233 (199).

perfectly authentic and personally undergone by him, Rimbaud saw multiple other experiences appear and diverge in all directions; these experiences were not real ones but purely hypothetical. In the place of a single form, other, often unexpected forms would assemble, like a kind of irregular rose window. Thus the poet's vision, endlessly dividing the facets it presented, became from moment to moment both richer and more numerous.

In Rimbaud, this phenomenon is particularly manifest in his use of colors. In his works, colors never seem to blend into a homogenous whole, in which the most important task would be the arrangement of hues and demitints. The canvases Rimbaud most often tries to create with words do not display—unlike those of Delacroix contemplated by Baudelaire—a background or general overtone of color, which might unify, or harmonize with, the disparity of the different strokes that come together in the painting. On the contrary. Apparently, for the author of *Illuminations* the purpose of colors is to avoid unification. They arrange themselves—one could even say, flatten themselves—next to each other, such that they seem to grow by their contrasts, their vividness, and their originality; yet finally, thrown together as they are, they make up a whole, but a heteroclite one.

There are many examples:

> From your black Poems—Juggler!
> White, green and red dioptrics,
> Let strange flowers burst forth
> And electric butterflies!

> *De tes noirs poèmes,—Jongleur!*
> *Blancs, verts et rouges dioptriques,*
> *Que s'évadent d'étranges fleurs*
> *Et des papillons électriques.*[131]

> —And will I see the yellow wood and the bright valley?
> The blue-eyed Bride, the man with the red brow, O Gaul,
> And the white Paschal Lamb, at their dear feet.

> *—Et verrai-je le bois jaune et le val clair,*
> *L'Epouse aux yeux bleus, l'homme au front rouge, ô Gaule,*
> *Et le blanc Agneau Pascal, à leurs pieds chers.*[132]

> In the morning when with Her, you fought in those shimmerings

131. "Ce qu'on dit au poète à propos de fleurs," 120 (113).
132. "Michel et Christine," 175 (129).

of snow, the green lips, the ice, the black flags and blue
rays, and the red perfumes of the polar sun.—Just
your strength.[133]

Pieces of yellow gold sown on the agate, mahogany
pillars
supporting an emerald dome, bouquets of white satin
and delicate
stalks of rubies surround the water-rose.[134]

Like a god with large blue eyes and a snow body, the sea
and
the sky entice to the marble stairs the swarm of young,
strong roses.[135]

No matter what the meaning of these various passages, no
matter the role they can play in the more or less delirious representation of a certain reality or, even more frequently, in the
invention of a wholly fictitious landscape, it is emminently clear
that the different colors almost simultaneously displayed here
are neither coordinated nor well matched. They are content, on
the one hand, with being merely juxtaposed and, on the other,
with forming a mass.

These colors then constitute what is with accuracy termed a
"medley" (*bariolage*). It is a word used by Rimbaud himself:

Fairy procession. Yes, wagons loaded with animals of
gilded wood, poles, and gaily-striped cloth, [toiles
bariolées] to the gallop of twenty spotted circus
horses . . .—twenty vehicles embossed, with flags
and flowers. . . [136]

In this description both multicolored and multiform, of a real
object—a circus or a procession—one notes the violently variegated quality of the details, and the impression of numerousness
which they suggest. The rest of the passage—too lengthy to be
cited here in its entirety—becomes confused and even funereal.
Coffins file by, "rolling along to the trot of large blue and black
mares." A certain disorder enters into the picture. This is a text
that deliberately accentuates the distortion of reality created by so

133. *Illuminations*, "Métropolitain," 291 (245).
134. *Illuminations*, "Fleurs," 285 (235).   135. Ibid.
136. *Illuminations*, "Ornières," 275 (239).

motley and discordant an event as a circus on full parade. The impression made upon the reader of this text is that the jostling about of colors and shapes allows for the portrayal—or, more precisely, for the *creation,* quite literally, in such a text—not of a multiplication of the real but, rather, the opposite: the fragmentation of everything that had seemed gathered into a whole. It is a fragementation, however, that does not appear here as the abrupt shattering of an object first perceived in its entirety and then suddenly reduced to a scattering of disconnected debris. On the contrary, as is so often the case in Rimbaldian poetry, at the moment things reveal themselves we discover that they have begun an ineluctable process of disintegration. Such is the effect—perhaps invisible, but surely disconcerting—of this poetry; an effect not so much final as terminal. The multiplication of elements composing it tends to transform itself into its opposite: that is, into a division. The components of the scene we witness, as they increase in number, dissociate themselves instead of continuing to amalgamate. The more things and shapes we find in the text, the more, assuredly, the globe containing them swells; but also, the less they hold together.

The same procedure of disunifying multiplication is seen again, albeit to perhaps a lesser degree, in another facet of the world (both real and imaginary) described by Rimbaud. I am referring to the theme of swarming (*fourmillement*). It appears very early in Rimbaud, in "Soleil et chair," for example. In this poem, the universe is perceived almost simultaneously, either in the infinity of the germinations that inhabit it or in the infinity of the spaces that embody it. But in both cases Rimbaud confronts us with a swarming universe:

> . . . it contains, big with sap and rays of light,
> The vast swarming of all embryos!

> . . . *Il renferme, gros de sève et de rayons,*
> *Le grand fourmillement de tous les embryons.*[137]

Rimbaud, moreover, asks himself the following question:

> Why the golden stars swarming like sand?

> *Pourquoi les astres d'or fourmillant comme un sable?*[138]

---

137. "Soleil et chair," 40 (27).   138. Ibid., 43 (31).

Elsewhere, the very interiority of beings appears to fall prey to this both infinite and minuscule agitation:

> My heart and my flesh kissed by your flesh
> Seethe with the putrified kiss of Jesus!
>
> *Et mon cœur et ma chair par ta chair embrassée*
> *Fourmillent du baiser putride de Jésus!*[139]

Let us also remember, in that singular poem called "Les Chercheuses de poux," the swarming of the lice eggs, perhaps indirectly suggested by the image that follows: "the white swarm of indistinct dreams." It is an image that recurs in another poem of the same period: "O your brow teeming with nits!"[140]

If swarming plays the role we are suggesting in Rimbaldian writings, it is because it reveals the general phenomenon of piecemealing to the infinitesimal, which never ceases being manifest and accentuated by our author. Swarming, streaming, shivering, rustling—these are the most frequent images the poet employs to make us feel the kind of reduction to its most minuscule parts to which, in Rimbaud, the world (and an interior existence) submits. It is where, as activity multiplies, it also divides into parcels of increasingly smaller proportions. Almost the polar opposite of Hugo, who indeed loves huge figures moving in a world that grows ever more immense, Rimbaud likes to grasp things and beings in the accumulation of elements ever less perceptible as if they were overcome by a serious illness that was nothing other than a phenomenon of decomposition, generalized universally.

15

THIS PHENOMENON IS NOT solely physical. It is, above all, mental. It is thought itself (the poet's thought, of course, primarily; but also that of the reader, who is caught up in the same circle) which, transformed into an infinity of parcels composed of words, fig-

---

139. "Les premières communions," 125 (101).
140. "L'Homme juste," 113 (105).

ures, detached and continually floating ideas, begins to whirl around in the mind. A common impulse sweeps along this confused mass in a sort of interior gyration, quite similar to that produced by running water moving in circles within a chasm that will ultimately engulf it. Marcel Raymond has put it this way: "Rimbaud's imagination is par excellence the place where natural, whirling forces are expressed."[141] Among the images that seem to have haunted the poet the most, there is one that recurs frequently, which may represent the deep movement of his inner life better than any other image. It is the whirlwind—a motion that shoots forward into one direction only to incurvate instantly, returning to its point of departure. This image appears in an early poem that I have cited a number of times: "Les Etrennes des orphelins." In this poem, two sleeping children dream of imaginary objects:

> In some strange dream when you saw toys,
> Candies dressed in gold, sparkling jewels,
> Whirling and dancing a sonorous dance
> Then disappearing under curtains, and reappearing!

> *Dans quelque songe étrange, où l'on voyait joujoux,*
> *Bonbons habillés d'or, étincelants bijoux,*
> *Tourbillonner, danser une danse sonore*
> *Pour fuir sous les rideaux, puis reparaître encore!*[142]

In this particular case, air serves as the medium through which dream objects can pursue their whirlwind course. But more often in Rimbaud, in the dreams and poems of his maturity, it is water that has this role—water preferably from an ocean stream, water moving in a circle inside a vast funnel. One is reminded of the "burning funnels,"[143] in "Le Bateau ivre" and, in particular, of the "thick Maelstroms,"[144] which, like the moaning of the Behemoths, can be heard fifty leagues away. There can be no doubt that here Rimbaud is thinking of the gigantic funnel described in a famous Edgar Allen Poe story, *A Descent into the Maelström*. It is the story of a young fisherman in his boat, who suddenly discovers that he is caught in a great conical abyss created by the tide, the sea streaming along the walls of the funnel: "Never shall

141. Marcel Raymond, *Vérité et poésie*, 219.
142. "Les Etrennes des orphelins," 36 (11).
143. "Le Bateau ivre," 130 (119).   144. Ibid.

I forget the sensations of awe, horror, and admiration with which I gazed about me. The boat appeared to be hanging, as if by magic, midway down, upon the interior surface of a funnel vast in circumference." The circular hole in which the fisherman is a prisoner is formed of walls moving with unbelievable speed, strewn with an infinity of objects of every sort: "fragments of vessels, large masses of building timber and trunks of trees, with many smaller articles, such as pieces of house furniture, broken boxes, barrels, and staves." This is the image both immense and confused of Edgar Allen Poe, whom Baudelaire translated; an image to which Rimbaud seems to have returned on several occasions—for example, when he once took a boat ride:

> The swaying motion on the bank of the river falls,
> The chasm at the sternpost,
> The swiftness of the hand-rail,
> The huge passing of the current
> Conduct by unimaginable lights
> And chemical newness
> Voyagers surrounded by the waterspouts of the valley
> And the current.

> *Le mouvement de lacet sur la berge des chutes du fleuve,*
> *Le gouffre à l'etambot,*
> *La célérité de la rampe*
> *L'énorme passade du courant*
> *Mènent par les lumières inouïes*
> *Et la nouveauté chimique*
> *Les voyageurs entourés des trombes de val*
> *Et du ström.*[145]

We can attribute this passage to Poe with near certainty—and to some maritime or river experience of Rimbaud's himself—because there is the use of the Germanic word *Ström;* the word used constantly by Poe in his own text to designate the Norwegian whirlpool, the Maelström. To this we can add the fact that the Ström's funnel, in the American storyteller's version, is strewn with multiple and, more often than not, fragmentary objects, which the current drags along the funnel formed by the walls. It is tempting to see in this image, at once grandiose and complex, a prefiguration of the strangely troubling landscape

145. *Illuminations,* "Mouvement," 304 (251).

that Rimbaud was to contemplate when he looked down into his inner world: a landscape also in the form of a whirling vacuum with images, figures, and ideas passing at breakneck speed along its sides, flooded by a strange light. Is this not the kind of imagination (probably inspired by Poe's vision) that produces, for example, the following poetic fragment:

> And the huge ruts of the ebb tide,
> Flow circularly toward the East,
> Toward the pillars of the forest,
> Toward the poles of the pier,
> Whose angle is struck by whirls of light.

> *Et les ornières immenses du reflux*
> *Filent circulairement vers l'est,*
> *Vers les piliers de la forêt,*
> *Vers les fûts de la jetée,*
> *Dont l'angle est heurté par des tourbillons de lumière.*[146]

This text shows us Rimbaud fascinated by a circular movement of waters that illuminate whirling spurts of light. As always, we see him metamorphose this external landscape into an interior one. Outside, inside, the same circular motion is effected with dizzying speed. The same is true, it would seem, of a phrase found in another poem. In it there is mention of "the whirling and leaping noise of conch shells and nights of men."[147] Whirling and leaping—are these not the two fundamental movements of Rimbaldian poetry? Of these two movements, the one that seems primary consists of leaping, spurting. It represents the awakening of the individual, the free energy of creative thought that transforms the world and itself as it pleases. The other movement is whirling, the incessant entry of thought into a cycle of ideas or images, a cycle whose circuitous route it must follow at an increasingly breath-taking speed, with no possibility of escape—unless one breaks the circle with a final leap and goes off tangentially, this time forever.

146. *Illuminations,* "Marine," 287 (235).
147. *Illuminations,* "Mystique," 283 (249).